Amazing Dads!
Fatherhood
Curriculum

WORKBOOK

Amazing Dads!
Fatherhood
Curriculum

Dan Griffin

Harrison Crawford

Published by John Wiley & Sons, Inc., Hoboken, New Jersey.
Published simultaneously in Canada.

For general information on our other products and services or for technical support, please contact our Customer Care Department within the United States at (800) 762-2974, outside the United States at (317) 572-3993 or fax (317) 572-4002.

Wiley also publishes its books in a variety of electronic formats. Some content that appears in print may not be available in electronic formats. For more information about Wiley products, visit our web site at www.wiley.com.

Library of Congress Cataloging-in-Publication Data applied for:

Set ISBN: 9781394239962

Paperback: 9781394239948

ePDF: 9781394240487

ePub: 9781394239955

Cover Design: Wiley
Cover Image: © LeoNiL/Shutterstock

Set in 11/16pt Palatino by Straive, Pondicherry, India

SKY10071457_040124

CONTENTS

ABOUT THE *AMAZING DADS!* PROGRAM

Congratulations on starting the *Amazing Dads!* program. Our guess is that you are already *amazing*! Our hope is that you will find tools in this program that will allow you to be even more *amazing* and maybe even confirm for yourself just how *amazing* you are.

 Amazing Dads! is a program unlike any other. It is the first truly trauma-informed parenting curriculum tailored specifically for fathers. It is important to recognize that as a father, you have different needs, face different challenges, and want different guidance with parenting than mothers do. This program addresses that reality in a way that you will hopefully find both comforting in the way it speaks to you as a man and a father and challenging in that you will be asked to do a great deal of self-reflection. The goal of *Amazing Dads!* is to help you create a vision of the father you want to be and to provide you with the awareness, tools, and confidence to achieve that vision.

 This program is designed to be trauma informed. That means that the language, activities, and tools throughout the program are meant to be challenging but in a way that is safe. Everything in the program was designed with an assumption that all participants have experienced some level or form of trauma in their lives, and creating an environment of safety for all participating dads was a top priority when creating the program. Trust and safety are key to creating lasting changes and becoming the father you want to be. Whether you have experienced trauma in your life or not, the trauma-informed approach is designed to create a safe environment for you to do the work that will help you become the father you want to be.

 You are reading this because you have decided to make (or are considering making) fundamental changes in how you show up as a father. In most cases, you will be using this workbook as part of a program in which you meet regularly with a group of other fathers. As part of this process, you will attend 18 meetings with these other fathers and all of you will have opportunities to develop new skills and new ways of thinking about yourself, your children, your families, and about fatherhood. One of the most powerful aspects of this program is the group setting where you will get to see just how common many of the issues are that fathers face but also to explore important differences that make each father unique and able to offer diverse perspectives. Again, the organization of the program is designed to make this group setting safe and trusting in a way that many fathers have not had the fortune of experiencing.

Topics covered in this program include:

- The impact of male socialization on boys, men, and fathers (a core theme that guides the whole curriculum).
- Trauma, how it shows up in men and fathers, and the importance of addressing any trauma history you might have.
- Skill-building and practical tools you can use with, and teach to, your children.
- Relationship skill development.
- Developing emotional understanding, particularly as relates to anger and shame.
- Enhanced communication skills for healthy conflict resolution.
- The influence of family of origin experiences.
- Exploring the relationships with fathers/father figures and mothers/mother figures.
- A candid exploration of sex, sexuality, and intimacy and how to begin having a healthy dialogue about these topics with your children.
- Differentiating discipline from punishment, how punishment can turn into abuse, and identifying what healthy discipline looks like.
- The effects of male socialization on the fathers' ability to create and maintain healthy relationships, offering them specific tools to help repair during times of disconnection.
- Finding balance and the importance of self-care as part of being a healthy father.
- Understanding and meeting the changing roles and expectations of men and fathers in the twenty-first century.

The hope is that your exploration of all these topics and your experiences will help you develop an idea of the father you want to be, whether that be confirming that you are already showing up in ways that align with the father you want to be, or identifying some changes you want to make to help align yourself with that vision of the father you want to be.

ABOUT THIS WORKBOOK

This workbook is meant for you to be able to record your experiences throughout this program. Using this workbook will help you reflect on and remember what you learn, think, and feel during the group meetings and as you continue to practice the tools you learn on your own between meetings. The workbook contains:

- Summaries of information you will receive in the group meetings.
- Many of the activities and exercises that you will do during the group meetings.
- Activities for you to work on between the group meetings.
- Space for you to reflect on what you learned in each session.
- A section where all of the grounding and relaxation exercises are listed so you have easy access to them whenever you might want to use one or refresh your memory of them.

The activities that are to be completed between the group meetings are designed to help you to reflect on what you have learned and to put some new skills and behaviors into practice. The "Into Action" exercises are meant to help you put what was discussed in the meeting directly into action in your own life. There are also additional Practical & Tactical exercises designed as deeper dives into the material and information discussed in the meetings. These are meant to be optional, additional ways you can explore the discussions and reflect on your own experiences.

Men tend to learn best by doing, and these activities also help you to see the benefits of what you are practicing. The activities are not things you have to do in order to pass a class. Some of them involve writing or drawing exercises, but your skills in these areas are not being tested. You do not need to worry about your handwriting or spelling. What matters is what you put into the activities and, consequently, what you get out of them. There are no right or wrong answers, no "shoulds" or "shouldn'ts," and your work will not be checked or graded. This workbook is a tool to help you with your growth toward the vision of the father you want to be, and something you can keep and look back on in the future to remind you of your growth and to use as a resource for things like grounding and relaxation exercises you will learn.

There will be opportunities during some of the group meetings for you to share what you have written in your workbook. You can share what you want and keep the rest private. The group meeting is a safe place, and there will be ground rules regarding confidentiality. If writing is difficult for you that is okay, you can draw pictures or simply make notes however works best for you.

You can use this workbook to highlight what you want to remember from each meeting and to make notes about what you are thinking and feeling as you go through this program.

You may be concerned about keeping your workbook private. If you live with others and are not sure they will respect your privacy, you should hide your workbook or lock it up. Or you can ask the facilitator or another trusted person to help you find a way to keep your workbook safe between group meetings. The facilitator is prepared for such requests. If the facilitator will be holding your workbook between meetings, he or she will respect your privacy and arrange for you to complete the extra activities after each meeting or at some other time.

Engaging the Father Within

Welcome! Congratulations on making the decision to work toward becoming the best father you can be. This is your first step toward becoming the Amazing Dad you have inside. Your first meeting in the *Amazing Dads!* program is an introduction to what you can expect throughout your participation in the meetings. There is discussion of the different goals of the program as a whole, and then you will have opportunities to explore your own goals for your time in the program as well as some important questions about what fatherhood means to you. This session is meant to "set the stage" for the rest of the program.

The goals of Meeting 1 are:

1. To discuss the structure of the program.
2. To go over the group agreements and expectations.
3. To explore what fatherhood means to you.
4. To commit to putting in the work to be the father you want to be.

Amazing Dads! Fatherhood Curriculum, Workbook, First Edition. Dan Griffin and Harrison Crawford.
© 2024 Dan Griffin and Harrison Crawford. Published 2024 by John Wiley & Sons, Inc.

Group Agreements

At the beginning of Meeting 1, your facilitator will explain some group agreements that will be maintained during each of the group meetings. Part of creating an environment of safety and trust in one another comes from each father committing to follow these agreements. The group agreements listed here are the common ones that are recommended, but the ones in your particular group may differ if there are specific requirements that the facilitator needs to follow.

Safety

We agree to create a safe space for everyone. This means physical safety, as well as a feeling of safety where each of us can share his experiences, opinions, and thoughts without fear of being shamed. We agree there will be no physical or verbal abuse. We agree to discuss any concerns for safety with the group facilitator(s).

Attendance & Participation

We agree to attend all meetings. If a conflict keeps us from being able to attend, we agree to contact the facilitator(s) ahead of time. We also commit to choosing to be on time for each meeting. We agree to participate and stretch outside our comfort zone as best we can, even if it is challenging. Also, each of us has a right to decide something is too uncomfortable to share and we agree to respect each dad's right to decide that for himself. We agree to keep focused on the topics of each meeting. We agree to help each other stay focused, including helping the facilitator(s) stay on topic.

Confidentiality

We agree to keep everything that is said in this group, in this group. We will not discuss the experiences or information shared by other dads outside this group. We are responsible for keeping the confidentiality in the group. We understand any limits to confidentiality on the part of the facilitator(s) will be explained to us as appropriate.

Respect

We agree to respect each other – our time, our experiences, and our challenges. We do not have to agree all the time, but when we disagree, we will do so while respecting the other's experience. We agree to share the time in this group, showing others respect by allowing each dad opportunities to share and participate. We agree to show respect by being honest when we choose to share as well as when we give feedback to others.

Amazing Dads! Fatherhood Curriculum

Other (feel free to write any others that your facilitator or group identifies here):

There are times when you may feel uncomfortable, anxious, or frustrated in the group. This happens to everyone at times, especially in unfamiliar settings and with new experiences. Many of us keep these feelings to ourselves as we have not learned how to deal with excitement, anxiety, and feeling uncomfortable in ways that are healthy. Throughout your time in this program, you will learn many different techniques that you can use to help you relax, calm yourself, and feel more grounded. The first two techniques (the ones you learned in Meeting 1) are listed here, and there is also an Appendix at the back of this workbook where *all* the techniques are housed for your reference later.

Box Breathing

This exercise can help you calm your body and your mind quickly and efficiently:

1. Put one hand on your chest and the other on your stomach.
2. As you take a few breaths, notice which hand is moving more. Try moving your breath deeper into your lower abdomen, so that your hand on your stomach moves more as you breathe.
3. Close your mouth and press your tongue lightly to the roof of your mouth. Let your jaw relax.
4. Take in a full breath slowly through your nose, counting to four.
5. Hold your breath, counting to four.
6. Exhale all the air through your mouth, counting to four.
7. Rest for a count of four.
8. As thoughts come up, acknowledge them, and then return your focus to your breathing and counting.
9. Go through three more rounds of this breathing on your own, slowly breathing in through your nose for four counts, holding for four counts, breathing out through your mouth for four counts, and resting for four counts.

Deep breathing can be helpful when dealing with feelings of anger, stress, fear, panic, or any other uncomfortable feelings. Plus, it is generally healthier to take controlled, deep breaths versus shallow ones. The more you practice this way of breathing, the more natural it will become for you.

Palms Up, Palms Down

This exercise can help you move aside anything that is weighing on your mind, or even any physical discomfort, in order to allow you to focus your mind on the present.

1. Sit up straight in your seats, with both feet on the floor and your eyes focused on your hands.
2. Hold both your arms outstretched, with your palms side by side and facing up as if someone was about to put something in your hands. Make sure you don't rest your arms on anything, they should be out in front of you in the air.
3. Visualize any thoughts, feelings, and stresses bothering you right now.
4. Now imagine placing all of your stresses, problems, troubles, and anything bothering you into your hands. These emotions and thoughts are out of your bodies and lying in your hands. Picture them there.
5. Go back inside yourself and find any remaining pain, discomfort, and stress. Then slowly feel these sensations move out through your arms and into your hands.
6. Imagine the weight of holding all these problems, difficult thoughts and emotions, and physical distress in your hands. Feel the strain of carrying them and the weight pushing down on your hands.
7. Now, slowly turn your hands upside down letting your palms face the floor. Let all the problems, stresses, difficult feelings, and negativity fall to the floor. For now, drop your burdens.

All these problems have not disappeared or been resolved, but you have chosen to put them down for the time being to be able to focus on what you need to.

Consider practicing Box Breathing and Palms Up, Palms Down exercises between the meetings. Like any new skill, the more you practice these exercises, the more efficient you will get at using them and the more effective they can be at helping you calm your body and your mind.

A big part of the *Amazing Dads!* program is building a vision of the father you want to be and the ways you want to show up for your kids and as a father. One of the first exercises is to begin thinking about what you want to get out of going through this program. Whether you have been told you need to go through this program or you are participating voluntarily, you have an opportunity to think about what you can get out of this experience to help you as a father.

Expectations – What Do You Want to Get Out of This Group?

There may be many reasons you choose to use this workbook and participate in this program. Whatever brought you to *Amazing Dads!*, it is important to consider what *you* want to get out of your participation. Consider what you want to get out of your time doing this important work, and how you want to use this work to become the father you want to be.

What is the work that *you* are here to do to become the best father you can be? What are some things you would like to learn through this process?

Feel free to write down your answers here:

What Is Fatherhood to You?

You may not have had an opportunity to think about this before. It may sound like a simple thought, but there is value in taking some time to answer the following questions:

1. What does fatherhood mean to you?

2. What does being a dad mean to you?

3. What are some of the positives of being involved as a dad? Think about positives for you and positives for your children.

4. What is one of the toughest parts of being a dad?

5. What do you enjoy most about being a dad?

Commitment to Conscious Fatherhood

"I commit to practicing what I learn. I will do my best to let go of wanting to do this perfectly. Instead, I will consciously practice being the best father I can be."

This commitment is incredibly important to your growth as a father. It shows that you are willing to try new things with an open mind. It also means that you agree to be kind to yourself and give yourself grace in your efforts – it is not about perfection, but rather using the things you learn in a conscious way, making purposeful choices about how you show up as a dad.

Next, you will find the first Into Action and Practical & Tactical exercises of the program. These are meant to be completed between meetings to practice parts of what was learned in each meeting. The Practical & Tactical exercises are a chance to do a deeper dive into what was discussed in each meeting.

Into Action: Values Clarification – What Is Important to You?

Part of being the best dad you can be is thinking about what you personally find important – your values – and making a conscious decision to act in ways to live by those values. Just as importantly, you will want to act in ways that align with your values as a way of passing those values down to your children.

Look at the list of possible values on this page. Take a few minutes to read through all of them and pick your top 10. Number your top 10, with number 1 being the most important to you. Feel free to identify any values you hold that are not on the list, using the blank spaces provided.

Love	Wealth	Respect
Family	Morals	Stability
Success	Knowledge	Fairness
Power	Friends	Relaxation
Free time	Adventure	Peace
Variety	Calmness	Wisdom
Freedom	Fun	Creativity
Recognition	Nature	Safety
Popularity	Responsibility	Beauty
Honesty	Humor	Spirituality
Loyalty	Reason	
Independence	Achievement	

Please answer the following questions:

1. The values I *would like* to live by are. . .

2. The values I *actually* live by are. . .

3. The values I would like my children to learn from me are. . .

4. Three things I can do to promote these values to my children are. . .
   a.

   b.

   c.

Hopefully, you have a clearer picture of the values you find important and want to instill in your children.

Next is the first Practical & Tactical exercise. These exercises or activities are also meant to be completed between meetings. They offer opportunities to explore the topics discussed in the meetings on a deeper level to help you continue to take on the information you learned in each meeting.

Practical & Tactical

Have a conversation with your children about what you value and what is important to you. This conversation can vary based on the age of your children but share what you learned about yourself and your values in the assignment with your children.

Have this conversation with your partner, co-parent, a family member, or a trusted friend as well.

Ask your children about their values. Even at a young age, teaching a child to be aware of what is important to him or her is a helpful exercise.

Meeting 1 Summary

Congratulations on your commitment to becoming the best father you can be!

After participating in this first meeting, you should have a better sense of what to expect from the *Amazing Dads!* program. You spent time discussing some group agreements that will help everyone create a group that is safe, open to different ideas and opinions, and where you are accountable to yourself and your fellow dads, and they are accountable to you in return.

You also learned three different grounding and relaxation exercises: Box Breathing, Palms Up/Palms Down, and In With The Good Breathing. You will have many opportunities to practice these during the upcoming meetings, plus you will learn even more throughout the rest of the program. The hope is that you will continue to build your toolbox of skills in order to feel more confident in your ability to care for yourself in times of distress. Remember, there is a section at the back of this workbook where you can find *all* the exercises you will learn, so you can easily find whatever you may need.

Throughout your time in this program, you will learn many skills, be exposed to new ideas, and have many opportunities to think about and practice how you might use this new information in your life and with your children. Congratulations on taking the first step toward becoming an Amazing Dad!

The Man Rules

While all meetings in this program are important, *this* meeting is one that sets the stage for all of the *Amazing Dads* program! In this meeting, you will learn about how the ways that boys are raised make a huge impact on how they see the world, how they see what is safe for them or not, and how they relate to others in their lives. You will discuss how many of the "rules" for boys and men are often pressed upon them in harmful ways, and how those rules push boys and men away from healthy connections with others. The result is that many boys and men feel safer when they stick to the rules that are actually harmful to them. And that has a big impact on how you show up as a father whether you realize it now or not.

The goals of Meeting 2 are:

1. To better understand your ideas about masculinity and being a man.
2. To better understand the qualities of healthy fathering.
3. To look at typical messages about being a man and how they help or harm your experience of being a father.

Amazing Dads! Fatherhood Curriculum, Workbook, First Edition. Dan Griffin and Harrison Crawford.
© 2024 Dan Griffin and Harrison Crawford. Published 2024 by John Wiley & Sons, Inc.

Part of the opening for each meeting moving forward will include the "Feelings and Body Check-In." This is a way to begin recognizing your own emotional state *in the moment*, which is something many dads are not used to thinking about. To help you identify new feeling words, you can find a list of examples below to choose from.

Examples of Feelings

Angry	Joyful
Sad	Anxious
Thoughtful	Nervous
Happy	Afraid
Amused	Hurt
Bitter	Jealous
Calm	Lonely
Mad	Content
Miserable	Disappointed
Pleased	Discouraged
Depressed	Relieved
Embarrassed	Grateful
Grieving	Ashamed

The next activity asks you to consider the rules about what it means to be a "real" man. Not all of the Man Rules are negative or harmful. However, there are many that are. They limit men and dads, encouraging disconnection, lack of self-awareness, and even sometimes harmful behaviors. The next activity will help you identify the rules as you experience them as well as how they do or do not line up with your ideas about what it means to be a healthy father.

The Man Rules:

What are the "rules" for being a man?

This next activity has you explore what it takes to be a healthy father. What types of expectations, behaviors, and so on are needed to be able to be a healthy father?

The Components of Healthy Fathering:

- What are the components of being a healthy father?

Subgroup Discussion: The Man Rules vs. Healthy Fathering

Now that you have explored the Man Rules and also the components of what it means to be a healthy father, please answer the following questions in your subgroup.

- Which of the Man Rules *support* being a healthy father?

- Which of the Man Rules *do not* support being a healthy father?

You spent this meeting considering what "Rules" you learned about masculinity growing up and how they do or do not line up with the skills it takes to be a healthy father. After each meeting, you will be invited to explore some additional activities that will help you use this information in your life outside of the group. Please take some time to complete the following activities before your next meeting.

Into Action

Part 1: Choose three of the Man Rules that you can relate to, and that *support* being a healthy father. Write about how those Rules have helped you as a father. Share what you have written with your partner or a trusted friend.

Part 2: Choose three of the Man Rules that you can relate to, but that *do not* support healthy fathering. Write about how those rules have hindered you as a father. What are three ways you can do things differently when it comes to these rules, so that they have less of an impact on you? Share what you have written with your partner or a trusted friend.

Practical & Tactical

Write out a list of Man Rules or Woman Rules (depending on the gender of your child or children) you are comfortable exploring with your children. Discuss these rules with them. Give them the opportunity to learn about what the rules are and where they come from to become more conscious of them and to choose what is best for them. Give them the choice in this that you were not given. After you have the discussion, write a little about what it was like, what went well, and what didn't. If you are not comfortable having this discussion with them, write down ways you can consciously act and model the rules you want them to learn from you. If applicable, discuss this with your partner, significant other, or co-parent.

Meeting 2 Summary

After finishing this meeting, it should be clear that much of what we believe about masculinity and what being a "real" man really means comes from our upbringing and the messages we got from parents, teachers, peers, coaches, and the media. This is true for all people, but for boys and men it often turns out to be damaging because many of the messages we receive are often unhealthy and "taught" to us in ways that are hurtful.

As you recognize what messages and Man Rules you absorbed, you now have an opportunity to decide for yourself what you do with that knowledge. We encourage you to use this new awareness to help you make decisions about how you want to show up as a man and as a father. The Man Rules were not gifted to you by choice, but the beauty of learning about this is that *you* now have the choice about how you move forward. Even more importantly, now have better information to influence how your kids grow and learn about these rules.

It is important to remember that the goal in using this new information is not that you will use it perfectly and make only the "right" choices all the time. Rather, the goal is to use this information and be conscious of what influences you so you can change your thinking, change your actions, and become the father you want to be. This is what is called conscious masculinity and conscious fatherhood.

Toxic Water

This meeting continues on the theme of the Water and highlighting many ways culture strongly influences how we understand the world around us. This is especially true when it comes to how we perceive others, specifically people who are different from us. It is important to explore these ideas for multiple reasons: to begin thinking about how your own culture fits into the larger system (or doesn't fit in), to get honest about the ideas, beliefs, and judgments you have internalized about other people and groups, to imagine ways you can use your culture to create more equality and understanding among the people in your lives, and to consider how you can help your children see their own power in celebrating differences and recognizing the value of diversity.

The goals of Meeting 3 are:

1. To better understand the systemic impact of patriarchy and the toxic culture of masculinity as they relate to the trauma that men can experience and perpetuate.
2. To better understand how the unique experiences of trauma are influenced by the intersection of culture, race, class, and gender.

Amazing Dads! Fatherhood Curriculum, Workbook, First Edition. Dan Griffin and Harrison Crawford.
© 2024 Dan Griffin and Harrison Crawford. Published 2024 by John Wiley & Sons, Inc.

3. To look at how privilege and entitlement create disconnection and harm in our relationships and our communities, and to highlight how to use this awareness to make positive changes personally and for our children.

Skills for being able to imagine what someone else is going through are desperately needed in order to have a positive impact on the world and those we interact with. Being able to imagine someone else's experience and feelings is called empathy. Building empathy is something you can promote in your children, and it starts with being able to put yourself "in the shoes" of someone else. This next activity focuses on being able to do that.

The Shoes of Another

Based on the description you received on your slip of paper, take some time to answer the following questions in your small group. There is space for you to take notes if you choose to.

1. What messages do you believe a child who fits this description has gotten from society?

2. In what ways, if any, do you think the messages changed as this person grew into an adult?

3. What kind of challenging experiences do you think this person may have had based solely on their characteristics?

4. What kind of messages do you believe this person has to share with their children about their identity and place in our society?

Now that you have spent time empathizing with someone very different from yourself, take some time to reflect on your own lived experiences by answering the following questions in your small group.

1. What kind of messages did you *receive* about your own identity from society as a child?

2. What kind of healthy messages do you *send yourself* about your identity?

3. What kind of unhealthy messages do you *send yourself* about your identity?

4. What kind of challenging experiences have you had *as a father* based on your personal characteristics?

5. What kind of challenging experiences have *your children* endured because of their personal characteristics?

Building empathy in yourself and in your children is one way to "cleanse the toxic water" that we all encounter. Healing can begin when people try to understand one another and empathize with each other's experiences.

Into Action: Reflections on Toxic Water

Please take some time to answer the following questions:

1. What messages did your parent(s) or caregiver(s) pass on to you regarding your identity and cultural characteristics?

2. What messages did you get from society about your identity and cultural characteristics?

3. What do you want your children to know about their own identity and cultural characteristics? Are they similar to what your parent(s) or caregiver(s) taught you? Are they different? Why?

4. How did you (or will you) respond to your children asking questions about their identity, culture, or privilege?

Practical & Tactical

In order to explore this subject even further, you are invited to have a conversation about these topics with one person in your life that you have never spoken to about this – a best friend, parent, mentor, other family members, etc. You are encouraged to share any insights you gained from the meeting, what you feel about what was discussed, anything that stood out to you as important, and also to ask the person you choose to talk to about her/his own thoughts on this information.

Meeting 3 Summary

During this meeting, you were introduced to the idea of Toxic Water. This refers to the biases, negative associations, and power imbalances that exist in our culture as part of the Water. Much of this program is about building awareness of things you may not have known before beginning this journey. This meeting focused on building awareness of the cultural and societal influences you and others experience and, depending on your own background, may negatively impact you and your children.

Dads and Trauma: Breaking the Cycle

This meeting focuses on a challenging topic, but one that is critical to explore as a father. Trauma is a topic that is being discussed more openly, and with the increase in research and knowledge over recent decades we are learning how important it is to understand what trauma is, how it shows up differently for different people (e.g., men versus women), and how critical it is to make sure to get help if you have any history of trauma.

This meeting is not meant to replace trauma-related treatment such as therapy or medication. It is important to understand that this is meant as an educational opportunity to explore what trauma is and to give you more insight into what trauma looks like for men and fathers.

As you go through this meeting, recognize what comes up for you. This can easily be a triggering discussion about a very serious topic. Therefore, checking in with yourself as you learn the information and go through the activities is important. You are learning different skills and tools to be able to care for yourself at any given moment, so remember that you have those skills to access anytime you begin to feel angry, upset, frightened, or just uncomfortable. Remember, you can always reach out to someone else for help or support as well.

The goals of Meeting 4 are:

1. To define trauma and learn how it can come from many different sources.
2. To become more aware of how trauma in fathers is impacted by the Man Rules.
3. To recognize how common trauma is and that it does not reflect upon who you are as a man.

The activity that comes next is meant to take whatever form works best for you. This is an opportunity to think about and express your life experiences in an artistic way, without having to write anything and without any specific requirements for how to complete it. You are invited to consider your life in different periods of time (e.g., childhood, adolescence, young adulthood, and adulthood) and create a representation of your experiences during those times that are meaningful for you. You are encouraged to use colors, images, and drawings, but go with your instinct on what will be best for you.

You will notice that the Into Action exercise that follows this meeting asks you to add to this particular artistic project in a unique way. Take your time on this and simply focus on making it meaningful to you.

Activity: The Colors of Life

Examples of Events That Could Result in Trauma (Black 2018)

The following are examples of events that can result in trauma for an individual. Please remember that everybody experiences events differently, so not all the examples listed are may be experienced as traumatic by every person.

Big-T Traumas may be responses to:

- War, invasion, attack, violent revolution, an act of terrorism, etc.
- Natural disasters such as floods, fires, hurricanes, landslides, etc.
- Rape
- Sexual or physical abuse
- Violence in the home
- Car, train, plane, or bus accidents
- Crime victimization
- Captivity
- Serious injury or illness
- Acts of racism
- Witnessing violence
- Chronic neglect, especially among children and the elderly
- The unexpected death of someone close to you
- Forced relocation, becoming a refugee, living in an internment camp, etc.

Small-t traumas may be responses to:

- Failing at something important to you
- Losses (the loss of a friend, a prized possession, a hoped-for promotion, etc.)
- High stress at work or school
- Harsh, unfair, or extreme criticism
- Rejection
- Being bullied
- Being shamed or demeaned
- Being yelled at
- Being ignored, disrespected, or discounted

- Betrayal
- Control or manipulation by someone you trust, especially an authority figure
- Discovering or witnessing the infidelity of your partner or parent
- Inconsistent or contradictory responses from a parent or partner
- A lack of empathy from a parent or partner
- Unrealistic expectations
- An acrimonious divorce
- Spiritual boundary violations (e.g., if someone uses his or her religious authority to control you or if you're sent for extensive training in a religion you don't believe in)
- Enmeshment (not being allowed to have your own thoughts, feelings, and desires)

Five Senses Mindfulness

The Five Senses Mindfulness exercise is a simple and effective way to practice being in the present moment, in the "here and now." Find a quiet place where you can practice this for about 5–10 minutes without interruption. As you go through the steps, take about 15–30 seconds in between to give yourself time to experience each sense.

1. *Hearing*: Spend a few moments focusing on what you hear. Notice the different sounds, perhaps ones you didn't hear initially. Suspend any judgment of them. They are neither good nor bad, they just are.
2. *Smell*: Shift your attention to any smells you pick up. Again, notice them without assigning any judgment of good or bad, just that they are.
3. *Touch*: Focus on your sense of touch. Notice the feeling of the fabric of your clothes, or wherever your hands are resting. Notice the sensation of sitting in the chair, your feet on the ground.
4. *Sight*: Concentrate on your sense of sight by just observing what is around you. There are many things you could notice, from the different shades of color to different textures of the objects around you. Avoid judging the sights, and just observe them and then move to the next one.
5. *Taste*: Shift your attention to your sense of taste. If you have a snack, feel free to take a small bite. If not, notice any taste inside your mouth now, or the taste of the air you're breathing, again suspending judgment.

The activity you are invited to complete before the next meeting uses the Colors of Life activity you started during the meeting and adds a component of resilience and healing. Read on for how you can make this activity even more meaningful.

Into Action: Kintsugi

Thinking about trauma and how it affects you can be a difficult idea to face. Dads often experience guilt or shame about past experiences that may have been traumatic. Many times, the Man Rules play into those feelings of guilt and shame, giving men and dads the idea that to acknowledge trauma is unmanly and weak. We challenged that in this meeting.

There is a Japanese art form called Kintsugi, where broken pottery is fixed using precious metal lacquer to mend the broken pieces together. This art does not try to hide blemishes and previous breaks but instead highlights them in a more beautiful way. The broken object then does not hide from its history but acknowledges it and understands that history, however, fractured, as a part of itself.

We have the opportunity to begin shifting how we view our past experiences. We can hide from them and bury them deep inside. Or we can recognize them as part of our history and work to mend ourselves in ways that will help us be brighter and more valuable than before.

With this in mind, your Into Action practice is to look over your Colors of Life project from this meeting. Identify where there may have been cracks in need of mending, or seams coming undone. Perhaps these relate to the more difficult times in your life, and where those fall on your paper. Next, fill those cracks or seams with positivity and hope. Perhaps for you that means drawing over the seams in your favorite color or using gold or silver colors to represent the value that can be added to your life through the process of beginning to heal. Or choose a different method to mend those cracks and seams that will still highlight the value and importance of doing so. You may have only one crack or seam to fix, or you might have many. Giving time and care to mending them is important for your journey as a conscious father.

You will not be asked to share this project with anyone, though you may choose to do so if you feel ready to share it with a trusted friend or partner. Be aware of what feelings come up for you when completing this project, including in the days after completing it. Practice some of the grounding and relaxation skills you have started learning in this program.

Practical & Tactical – Trauma Signs Self-Reflection

The following are some questions related to signs of trauma. Answer each question by circling the number, 1–5, that fits best for you:

• How often do you yell at other people or your children, or put them down in hurtful ways?

1-Never   *2-Rarely*   *3-Sometimes*   *4-Often*   *5-Always*

• How often do you find yourself mistreating your children and/or partner and sometimes feeling as though you are "possessed" or are two different people?

1-Never   *2-Rarely*   *3-Sometimes*   *4-Often*   *5-Always*

• When you feel close to someone, how often do you find yourself shutting down or becoming full of anger toward her or him?

1-Never   *2-Rarely*   *3-Sometimes*   *4-Often*   *5-Always*

• How often do you mock your children and/or partner or become uncomfortable when they cry or express vulnerability?

1-Never   *2-Rarely*   *3-Sometimes*   *4-Often*   *5-Always*

• When you feel sad or hurt, how often do you turn to anger or isolate in depression?

1-Never   2-Rarely   3-Sometimes   4-Often   5-Always

• How often do you overreact to conflict with extreme engagement or avoidance?

1-Never   2-Rarely   3-Sometimes   4-Often   5-Always

• How easily startled are you?

1-Never   2-Rarely   3-Sometimes   4-Often   5-Always

• How often do you find yourself struggling with violent reactions, thoughts, and fantasies?

1-Never   2-Rarely   3-Sometimes   4-Often   5-Always

• How often do you push others away with sarcasm, ridicule, or verbal abuse when they are getting too close?

1-Never   2-Rarely   3-Sometimes   4-Often   5-Always

• How often do you push away people you love and care about, using anger to protect yourself from being hurt?

1-Never   2-Rarely   3-Sometimes   4-Often   5-Always

• How often do you have nightmares of past experiences from your life?

1-Never   2-Rarely   3-Sometimes   4-Often   5-Always

Does any of this sound familiar to you? If so, it is just information, not a scientific assessment or diagnosis. However, it probably merits a conversation with a professional who understands trauma. You are not crazy, or a bad person. But you may need help to heal. Give yourself, and your loved ones, that gift.

Meeting 4 Summary

While this may have been a difficult meeting for you, the hope is that you now have a better understanding of what trauma is and how it shows up for men and dads. You learned how the Man Rules are often imposed on boys in traumatic ways, and then the Man Rules stop boys and men from wanting to seek help or support for what they are going through. Trauma is very complicated, unique to each person, and something that we still need to understand better.

Remember that you have multiple tools available to you to cope with any strong feelings or reactions to this meeting. This workbook contains all the different breathing, grounding, and relaxation exercises from the program, so use this as a resource to help you with any challenging reactions you have. You also have support available to you from your meeting facilitator(s), so reach out to him/her/them if you experience any difficulties, strong feelings, or confusion after this meeting.

As someone committed to being a conscious father, you have the opportunity to explore your own history and experiences and decide the best ways for you to heal. Remember: we repeat what we don't repair. You have a unique opportunity now to repair any hurt from your past, and this will help you to become the most amazing dad you can be.

Making the Connections – Mental Health, Addiction, and Trauma

This meeting continues on the theme of connecting our past history and experiences to our current reality. In this meeting, you will learn about the ways in which past challenging experiences still have the ability to impact you throughout your life. It is important to keep in mind, though, that this is simply information and not something designed to frighten you or increase your stress. When approaching this subject, you might find it helpful to consider how to use this information to better understand how you can be aware of the past's influence on you now, as well as think about ways to seek support for anything you may struggle with, now or in the future.

The goals of Meeting 5 are:

1. To explore the overlap of mental health challenges, addiction, and trauma through looking at the Adverse Childhood Experiences study.
2. To develop self-awareness of your needs in these areas, if any, and explore how to begin making positive changes.
3. To develop awareness of what needs your children might experience so you are prepared.
4. To explore your own resilience and ability to seek support to get your needs addressed as a way to help you become the best father you can be.

Amazing Dads! Fatherhood Curriculum, Workbook, First Edition. Dan Griffin and Harrison Crawford.
© 2024 Dan Griffin and Harrison Crawford. Published 2024 by John Wiley & Sons, Inc.

Adverse Childhood Experiences (ACEs)

The questionnaire that follows was created as part of the Adverse Childhood Experience study that was discussed in the meeting. Remember, this is just about collecting information about your experiences to help inform how you take care of yourself from now on. As you answer the questions, go with your first instinct, and do your best not to overthink how to answer.

While you were growing up, during your first 18 years of life:

1. Did a parent or other adult in the household often or very often: Swear at you, insult you, put you down, or humiliate you OR act in a way that made you afraid that you might be physically hurt?   YES   NO

2. Did a parent or other adult in the household often or very often: Push, grab, slap, or throw something at you OR hit you so hard that you had marks or were injured?   YES   NO

3. Did an adult or person at least 5 years older than you ever: Touch or fondle you or have you touch their body in a sexual way OR attempt or actually have oral, anal, or vaginal intercourse with you?   YES   NO

4. Did you often or very often feel that: No one in your family loved you or thought you were important or special OR your family didn't look out for each other, feel close to each other, or support each other?   YES   NO

5. Did you often or very often feel that: You didn't have enough to eat, had to wear dirty clothes, and had no one to protect you OR your parents were too drunk or high to take care of you or take you to the doctor if you needed it?   YES   NO

6. Was your mother or stepmother or father or stepfather: Often or very often pushed, grabbed, slapped, or had something thrown at her/him OR sometimes, often, or very often kicked, bitten, hit with a fist, or hit with something hard OR ever repeatedly hit for at least a few minutes or threatened with a knife or gun?   YES   NO

7. Were your parents ever separated or divorced?   YES   NO

8. Did you live with anyone who was a problem-drinker or alcoholic or who used street drugs or prescription drugs not as prescribed?   YES   NO

Amazing Dads! Fatherhood Curriculum

9. Was a household member depressed or mentally ill or did a household member attempt suicide?   YES   NO

10. Did a household member go to prison?   YES   NO

ACE Score (total of all "YES" answers): _____

Subgroup Discussion: Let's Get Real

Next, you have an opportunity to explore your own mental health and addiction needs in your small group. This is not an activity designed to create shame or judgment. Much of what is done in this program is meant to simply help give you awareness and get you thinking about these topics in ways you might not have before. Keep that in mind as you answer the following questions.

1. On a scale of one to ten, one being no concern at all, what is your level of concern for your own mental health? Why did you choose that rating?

2. On a scale of one to ten, how concerned do you think your *loved ones* are about your mental health? Why did you choose that rating?

3. On a scale of one to ten, what is your level of concern about potential addiction issues you may be experiencing? Why did you choose that rating?

4. On a scale of one to ten, how concerned do you think your *loved ones* are about potential addiction issues on your part? Why did you choose that rating?

5. What fears or concerns do you have about acknowledging and/or discussing these topics?

This is a new grounding and breathing exercise for you to practice and use. Practicing gratitude is shown to have real benefits for your mental health and any recovery you are working on in your life. Adding gratitude practice to some simple breathing creates a strong combination all in one brief exercise you can use.

Exercise: Gratitude Breathing

Take a minute or two to identify three things you are grateful for in this moment. They do not need to be "huge" things. Even the small things are worth your gratitude. Write these three items down here:

1.
2.
3.

Next, make yourself comfortable and prepare to do some deep breathing:

- Take a deep breath in through your nose, pause, and exhale fully through your mouth.
- Repeat this again.
- Now, with each full breath you take in through your nose, pause, and say one of your gratitude items to yourself either out loud or in your mind.
- After you state your gratitude, exhale your breath fully through your mouth.
- Take another full breath through your nose, but this time as you pause with your full breath in, say another one of your gratitude items to yourself.
- Exhale the full breath through your mouth.
- Repeat this a third time, saying your third gratitude item to yourself before you exhale fully.
- Take a couple of minutes to repeat this same process until you have repeated each of your gratitude items three times.

As you finish this breathing exercise, slowly return to the here and now.

Practicing gratitude can help build resilience. Even thinking about small things you are grateful for helps strengthen your "resilience muscles." Writing them down adds another layer to the positive effect that this can have.

This can also be turned into a cool activity to practice with your children. Have them practice gratitude – getting them to develop this habit now can have a big payoff throughout their lives!

This meeting may have challenged you, but the hope is that you recognize the importance of knowing how your experiences impact you (or might impact you in the future). Hopefully you also learned that you are fully capable of building resilience in yourself, as well as helping your children build resilience. The activity you're invited to complete before the next meeting involves thinking about the ways you can practice and build resilience. Consider involving your children in these activities as well to help them build good habits of their own.

Into Action: Resilience-Building Plan

As discussed in the meeting, resilience is a skill you can build just like working out a muscle. The more you use it and practice it, the more resilient you can become. Later, you will find multiple recommendations for how to practice resilience and continue building your resilience capacity. For this Into Action activity, you are encouraged to complete one section per day over the next week. You do not have to go in order but spending a few minutes each day will help you work on all the following areas to build resilience in a manageable way.

Recognize Your Signs of Stress

- Where do you feel stress in your body? (e.g., headaches, tense muscles in your neck, tightness in your chest, stomach aches)

- What are some of the unhealthy habits you engage in when feeling stressed? (e.g., overeating, using drugs or alcohol, not exercising)

- What are some of the positive habits you engage in when feeling stressed?

Focus on Building Physical Hardiness

- What kind of small changes can you invest in to improve your health? (e.g., better sleep, better nutrition, hydration, exercise, etc.)

- List one small change you can make now:

Strengthen the Relaxation Response – Calm Body and Calm Mind

- List some activities at home that could help you relax (Tip: there are many listed in your workbook if you want ideas):

- List some activities at work that could help you relax (Tip: there are many listed in your workbook if you want ideas):

- Try out some new relaxation skills such as mindfulness or meditation apps such as Calm or Headspace (not promoting these specifically, just offered as examples).

- Try some self-soothing activities such as:
  - Tactile (Holding something comforting or soothing)
  - Smell (Smell of lavender, fresh air)

- Visual (Puppy or kitten photos, looking out the window, etc.)
- Auditory (Listen to music, listen to sounds of nature)
- Taste (Drinking some tea, eating chocolate)

Identify and Use Your Strengths

- Describe a time when you were able to overcome or handle a major challenge in life.

- What did you learn about yourself?

- What personal strengths did you use?

- How might you apply these strengths now?

Increase Positive Emotions on a Daily Basis

- Identify sources of humor or joy.

- Express gratitude, visit someone, or write a letter.

- List your accomplishments.

Engage in Meaningful Activities

- Notice what happened in your day that was meaningful on a regular basis.

- What kinds of activities did you find meaningful?

- Identify activities that put you in the flow (Enjoyable things you do that cause you to lose track of time). List some of them below:

Counter Unhelpful Thinking

- Write down what you are thinking about when you get stressed and then ask the following:
  - What is the worst that can happen, and could I survive it?

  - What is the best thing that could happen?

  - What would I tell a friend in a similar situation?

- If you can't stop thinking about something, write about it a couple of times over a 4-week period for about 15 minutes each time. Notice how your story changes or your perspective becomes clearer each time.

- Remember a hero, a coach, or a mentor who encouraged you when you doubted yourself. Write about your experience with this person.

Create a Caring Community

- Surround yourself with positive and healthy people. Connect with friends and family on a regular basis (e.g., via phone, FaceTime, Zoom, in person).
  - When can you connect with them next? Put dates and times down below and try to stick to it.

- Identify your sources of support, at work, at home, and in the community. Who are your supports? List some of them here and keep adding to the list over time:

- Practice good communication and conflict resolution skills (more to come on these in the *Amazing Dads!* program).

Adapted from:
https://positivepsychology.com/resilience-activities-exercises/
#science-based-activities

Practical & Tactical: Complete the PACEs Questionnaire

Having answered the ACEs questionnaire in the meeting, we encourage you to take some time to answer a similar questionnaire, but one that has a very important difference: The questionnaire is called the Protective and Compensatory Experiences questionnaire because the questions ask about protective factors and positive events from your childhood.

When you were growing up, before your 18th birthday:

1. Did you have someone who loved you unconditionally (you did not doubt that they cared about you)?   YES   NO

2. Did you have at least one best friend (someone you could trust, had fun with)?   YES   NO

3. Did you do anything regularly to help others (e.g., volunteer at a hospital, nursing home, church) or do special projects in the community to help others (food drives, Habitat for Humanity)?   YES   NO

4. Were you regularly involved in organized sports groups (e.g., soccer, basketball, track) or other physical activity (e.g., competitive cheer, gymnastics, dance, marching band)?   YES   NO

5. Were you an active member of at least one civic group or a non-sport social group such as scouts, church, or youth group?   YES   NO

6. Did you have an engaging hobby – an artistic or intellectual pastime either alone or in a group (e.g., chess club, debate team, musical instrument or vocal group, theater, spelling bee, or did you read a lot)?   YES   NO

7. Was there an adult (not your parent) you trusted and could count on when you needed help or advice (e.g., coach, teacher, minister, neighbor, relative)?   YES   NO

8. Was your home typically clean AND safe with enough food to eat?   YES   NO

9. Overall, did your schools provide the resources and academic experiences you needed to learn?   YES   NO

10. In your home, were there rules that were clear and fairly administered?   YES   NO

Meeting 5 Summary

There are clear connections between adverse childhood experiences (ACEs), recent adverse experiences (something the ACE study did not include), and current or future mental health challenges and/or challenges with addiction. After participating in this meeting, you should have a better sense of how these things connect as well as a better understanding of your own experiences and how they may impact you today or in the future.

Negativity, shame, and judgment are major factors in the reluctance men and dads have over admitting to and seeking help for their mental health needs, and the stigma is equally bad (or worse) for individuals experiencing addiction. The problem is that the more we ignore it, the more it grows and causes problems on an individual level *and* in society as a whole. This meeting was designed to help you better understand how addiction, mental health, and trauma are connected and how being intentional about seeking support for any or all of those areas can have massive positive results for you and your children.

It's not all doom and gloom, though. This meeting also highlighted the idea of resilience and how you can build resilience for yourself and for your children. Resilience is another skill you can develop and use to offset the challenges you face in life. Part of being a conscious father is recognizing where you can direct your focus and energy that will have the most positive impact, and resilience-building is a worthy cause. As you think about what was discussed in this meeting, recognize that you are now armed with more information and an ability to use it for your benefit and for the benefit of your children.

MEETING 6

Feelings... Nothing More than Feelings

Meeting 6 begins an in-depth discussion about how fathers experience, deal with, and understand their own emotions and also how that translates to their parenting. We explore the anger funnel and begin to understand how the Man Rules often conspire to keep men angry and emotionally disconnected. You will learn a new tool called Digging Deeper that is an opportunity for you to be more real in our relationships, especially with our children. You will get the opportunity to look at mistakes you may have made with your children and how to do those same interactions differently with new tools of emotional awareness.

The goals of Meeting 6 are:

1. To take a deeper look at your emotions and the relationship fathers have with them.
2. To learn about anger and why it is the most common emotion associated with men and fathers.
3. To learn skills that can help you regulate your emotions and respond to them effectively.
4. To build skills that can help you teach your children about emotions and how to respond to their own feelings.

Amazing Dads! Fatherhood Curriculum, Workbook, First Edition. Dan Griffin and Harrison Crawford.
© 2024 Dan Griffin and Harrison Crawford. Published 2024 by John Wiley & Sons, Inc.

This meeting is the first with some new breathing and grounding exercises that are part of the check-in process. See those new exercises below. You can also find this at the back of the workbook in the appendix where all the grounding, relaxation, and breathing exercises can be found.

Exercise: Advanced Box Breathing

This exercise is an advanced version of box breathing, with counts going to six versus four.

1. Take a couple of normal breaths. Try moving your breath deeper into your lower abdomen.
2. Take a breath slowly through your nose, counting to six. One, two, three, four, five, six.
3. Hold your breath for a count of six. One, two, three, four, five, six.
4. Slowly exhale out your mouth as you count to six one more time. One, two, three, four, five, six.
5. Rest for six more counts before you start again. One, two, three, four, five, six.
6. Try it again.
7. As thoughts come up, acknowledge them and then return your focus to your breathing and counting.
8. Go through two more rounds of this box breathing on your own, counting to yourself.

The next exercise will probably be one you have not experienced before. It combines deep breathing with alternating tapping, which research has shown to help decrease feelings of anxiety and stress. It may feel strange at first, but give it time and practice and it might just become your favorite exercise!

Eagle's Wings Exercise

1. Take a few deep breaths from down in your abdomen.
2. Next, cross your hands across your chest so the tips of your middle fingers are just below your collarbone. The rest of your fingers will lay relaxed on your upper chest.
3. Try to have your fingers pointing up instead of outward. You can interlock your thumbs if this helps make it easier.

4. Now, slowly and steadily alternate tapping your hands on your chest repeatedly: right, left, right, left, resembling the flapping wings of an eagle.

5. Continue to take slow, deep breaths and continue tapping steadily.

6. Notice what is going through your mind and body: whether it be thoughts, images, feelings, or physical sensations.

7. Notice these things coming and going as you would watch clouds passing in the sky.

8. Continue breathing slowly and deeply.

9. Continue tapping: right, left, right, left, right, left.

10. When you feel in your body that you are relaxed, grounded, and it has been enough, you may stop.

If you want to know more about tapping and the positive effects it can have, a simple Internet search will give you information. If you search for "bilateral stimulation," you will find information that describes the science behind this exercise you just did.

The diagram you see below is an illustration of the Anger Funnel as it is discussed in this meeting. The image shows how feelings that are often uncomfortable for dads go into the funnel and come out the other end as some form of an anger response. This highlights how men and dads are trained to shy away from sitting with and expressing uncomfortable feelings, and instead we are trained to filter them out as anger which is the only "acceptable" feeling for men.

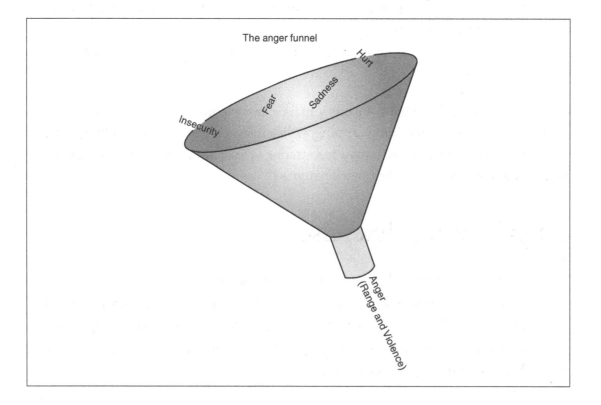

The anger funnel

Amazing Dads! Fatherhood Curriculum

Prompts for Digging Deeper Activity

Think about the most recent time you were angry with your children. Write your responses to the following prompts about that situation:

1. Describe the situation (who was there, what led up to it, any other details):

2. How did your anger show up? For example, was it raging, manipulation, or passive–aggressive?

3. How did you physically feel? Where in your body did you notice any physical sensations?

4. How did you act?

5. How did it affect you?

6. How did it affect the other person/people?

7. How did you feel afterward?

Discussion Points for Sharing Feelings Activity

Use the following prompts to help you in your discussion with your partner about the most recent time you became angry with your children.

1. Briefly describe to your partner the last time you became angry with your child.

2. Using the Anger Funnel concept, Dig Deeper and identify the primary emotion that was triggered by the situation you described. What was it?

3. Why is the primary emotion you identified difficult for you to *experience*?

4. Why is that emotion difficult for you to *express* to others?

5. What is an example of a time you were a boy and had that feeling? How were you treated?

6. In what way could you have responded to the situation from #1 differently?

7. "Do I owe any amends for my behavior?" Consider this: Do you need to clean up your behavior with your child(ren)? An amends is not simply an apology. An amends is taking responsibility with a commitment to change your behavior.

Optional Scenarios for Digging Deeper Activity

1. You have prompted your child three times to put his shoes on to be able to leave for school. Each time he has responded by saying, "Ok, I will," but he has not yet gotten his shoes on. You have to drop him off at school before heading to work, where you have an important meeting scheduled for right when you are supposed to be there. You are now running late. Describe what happens next using the prompts...

2. Your child has a habit of throwing things when she is upset. You have talked to her numerous times about how that is not appropriate behavior, but she continues to do it. Today you come home from a long day at work, and she asks you for ice cream. You tell her she has to wait until after dinner, and she immediately throws a book that is in her hands to the floor, breaking the cover off the book. She then starts to use a whining voice repeatedly saying, "I want ice cream now." Describe what happens next using the prompts...

3. You are putting your child's clothes into his drawers after doing laundry when you come across a bag of marijuana hidden in the drawer. You have made it clear before that there is no drug or alcohol use allowed. Just then, your child walks into the room. You ask him about the marijuana, and the response you get is, "At least I'm not shooting up meth." Describe what happens next using the prompts...

4. You are a single dad with a one-month-old baby. It is 3 am and you have not gone to sleep yet because your baby is crying and crying for seemingly no reason. The baby is fed, has a clean diaper, and does not seem to be sick. You hold the baby, rock the baby, and try everything you can think of to soothe the baby, but nothing is working. The baby keeps crying and crying. Describe what happens next using the prompts...

Activity: A Picture of Anger

This page gives you space to work on your depiction of what you experienced when your father (or father-figure, or another significant male presence in your life) was angry. You are invited to draw a picture of your experience. Please remember it is not about the quality of the art, but about giving you a chance to put your experience down in a creative form.

This next exercise is a guided imagery and grounding exercise that can be very powerful, especially after a challenging experience or discussion. You could use this on your own by recording yourself reading the script, or you could have someone read this to you in a calm, low voice.

Place of Peace Relaxation Exercise

1. Take a deep breath in while you silently count to four. One, two, three, four.

2. Now breathe out slowly, silently counting to four again. One, two, three, four.

3. Remember to breathe from your abdomen. Breathe in again. One, two, three, four.

4. And out again. One, two, three, four.

5. Now picture in your mind a place of peace. Maybe you have been there before or maybe it is a place of your dreams. Maybe it's your bed or a comfortable chair. Maybe it's sitting by a lake or lying in the sun by the ocean. Maybe it's a special place you visited as a child or a scene from one of your favorite movies. It may be a real place or an imaginary place. See that place in your mind.

6. Keep breathing slowly and deeply.

7. Let the muscles in your face relax.

8. Let your brow relax.

9. Let your jaw relax.

10. Let your neck and your shoulders relax.

11. Imagine all the tension draining out of them. Let it go.

12. Let your hands and arms go limp next to you.

13. Let your middle relax – your chest and your abdomen.

14. Keep breathing in and out.

15. Let your hips and your legs relax.

16. Let your feet relax.

17. Relax your whole body and imagine yourself in that favorite, safe place. This is your place of peace. You are safe in this place. Your life is the life you always wanted it to be. You are the loving and caring father you want to be.

18. Your life is full of peace. You are full of peace.

Amazing Dads! Fatherhood Curriculum

19. As you breathe in these next couple of times, breathe in the word "Peace."
20. As you breathe out, exhale all the pain from your past and all the negative feelings and thoughts.
21. Breathe in peace.
22. Breathe out pain.

Repeat the breathing process several more times.

Into Action

1. Ask your children to draw a picture of what *their* anger looks like. Have your children explain their drawing(s) to you.
2. Ask your children to draw a picture of what they experience when *you* are angry. Be prepared to discuss with your children no matter what they draw. Ask your children to explain their experiences to you.
3. With your children, each of you draw what you *would like* your children's experience to be when you are angry. Talk to them about how they respond to their own anger, and how you plan to respond to yours going forward.

Practical & Tactical

If you have not finished your drawing of what you experienced when your father (or stepfather, uncle, or another significant male presence in your life) was angry, please take the time to complete it. Once complete, share your drawing with someone you trust, ideally a male and perhaps your father or the person whom you drew about. Ask him about his experience with his father/father figure.

*** A brief note on this: sharing this with another man is strongly encouraged because we rarely have these types of discussions with other men, even those we are close to. Choosing to share this with another man opens the door to a deeper relationship with him than you might have with any man. It is also an example of how you can consciously choose to brush off any Man Rules that tell you that you have to avoid these conversations with other men.

Meeting 6 Summary

Developing comfort with exploring feelings and emotions is a big part of becoming a healthy, conscious father. As discussed in this meeting, men and dads are usually pushed to ignore their own emotional lives, to the point that many do not even learn how to properly understand their emotions or know how to label them. The messages we get from the Man Rules tend to be pretty clear: don't talk about feelings, but if you have to talk about or express them, then funnel every uncomfortable feeling out as anger. According to the Man Rules, this is the only way to "feel" and still be a "real man."

The problem (or one of them) is that this *doesn't work*. It might save you from feeling (or being perceived as) unmanly, but when you get into a relationship or if you want to be a healthy example for your children, this severe limitation of emotions will cause more problems. Healthy relationships require vulnerability, sharing of feelings, and the ability to repair hurt feelings. Raising children requires you to manage all sorts of difficult, changing, and confusing emotions for this little human who doesn't know how to manage them himself or herself.

This meeting challenged you to recognize your patterns when it comes to recognizing and interpreting your internal emotional experience. The anger funnel is a great way to understand what so many dads do with uncomfortable emotions, and it allows us to see that funneling everything out as some sort of anger response is harmful to us and those around us. As someone committed to conscious fatherhood, you have started to learn the tools for expanding your understanding of your emotional life which will translate into being better able to help your children do the same. You get to be the example for them, so embracing growth in your emotional intelligence is going to have positive impacts on your children no matter what.

MEETING 7

Exploring Family Dynamics – Past and Present

In this session, we first explore the Woman Rules, the other half of the Rules of Gender. While not everyone subscribes to the Rules of Gender, most individuals do (often without thinking about it), and it is important for men to understand what women have to live with and how they are expected to act and feel. Then we look at the impact your family had on your life and your experiences as a man and a dad. You will learn four common roles in families – hero, invisible child, scapegoat, and mascot – and begin to look at how the role you played in your family growing up has followed you into adulthood and may even be impacting how you show up as a father.

The goals of Meeting 7 are:

1. To learn some common patterns in family relationships and recognize how those patterns may show up in your current family.
2. To discover how your families of origin were influenced by the Man Rules and the Woman Rules, and also passed the rules down.
3. To use your creativity to develop a Family of Origin Project.

While this program is focused on dads, it is important to recognize that in addition to the Man Rules, there is messaging and pressure put on women with regard to femininity and we refer to that pressure as the Woman Rules. We must recognize that

Amazing Dads! Fatherhood Curriculum, Workbook, First Edition. Dan Griffin and Harrison Crawford.
© 2024 Dan Griffin and Harrison Crawford. Published 2024 by John Wiley & Sons, Inc.

men and women *both* have rules for how they "should" think, act, and feel in order to fit the gender scripts that our culture has for both sexes. The Woman Rules are just as powerful and can be just as harmful to women as the Man Rules can be to men. Therefore, we want to make sure to understand the common Woman Rules because that knowledge can help you better empathize with any women in your life.

Common Woman Rules

- Be thin – always
- Be beautiful – always
- Be a nurturer
- Be a mother
- Be in a relationship with a man – always
- Be weak
- Be emotional
- Be passive
- Be quiet
- Be nice
- Be domestic
- Be selfless
- Care for everyone other than yourself
- Be a lady in the streets and a freak in the sheets

Consider the ways that the Woman Rules are as limiting to girls and women as the Man Rules are for men and boys. Also, you might notice that the Woman Rules are nearly complete opposites of the Man Rules. If you think about it, this means that both men and women are only "allowed" to act in ways that are opposite of each other, and both sides have to miss out on the full human experience in order to conform to our culture's ideas about gender.

Descriptions of Common Family Roles

After going through the Family Sculpture activity, you should have a better understanding of some of the common roles that exist within many families. Here are the descriptions that were covered today so you have them to reference later.

Amazing Dads! Fatherhood Curriculum

Hero: The Hero is most often the first-born child in a family. The Hero takes on the role of making the family look good. He usually gets the best grades, excels in sports, and follows the rules of the family. He feels a lot of pressure to be perfect. He is expected to always represent the family in a positive way. The Hero can be at risk for emotional abuse due to significant and sometimes inappropriate responsibilities placed on him.

Scapegoat: The Scapegoat is usually the second-born child in a family. Since the Hero already has his role figured out and gets to be the one who excels at everything, the Scapegoat has to find other ways to get attention in the family. He usually figures out that he can do this through acting out. He rebels, does not follow the rules of the family, and in doing so distracts attention away from the real causes of the family's dysfunction – the unhealthy relationship between Dad and Mom. The Scapegoat usually has to turn to people outside the family for any sense of connection. He is more social with peers but is also more susceptible to peer pressure. The Scapegoat can be vulnerable to physical abuse due to his acting out tendencies.

Lost child: The Lost Child is usually the third-born child in the family. The Hero and the Scapegoat already get the lion's share of attention in the family, so the Lost Child tends to fade into the background as he cannot compete. He tends to keep to himself and is careful not to cause problems. He often focuses on reading, computers, video games, and other activities he can do on his own. The Lost Child can be at risk for sexual abuse due to his isolation.

Mascot: The Mascot is usually the last-born child. He tends to fill the role of family jester. He often gets attention by using humor or charm, but he can also be hyperactive. In healthy families, he tends to be well-cared for because he has many other siblings to play with, and because by their last child many parents have relaxed their parenting styles. However, in high stress families each additional child adds to the stress in the family. He is often more vulnerable to physical abuse due to his hyperactivity and the increased stress in the family.

Prompts to Help Create Your Family of Origin Project

Use the following prompts to help you create your Family of Origin Project:

1. Who will you include in your project? Which parent(s), caregivers, or siblings (if any)? Any extended family members?

2. What will you depict them doing? How can you depict what was going on in your family at the time?

3. Do the Man Rules show up in your project?

4. Consider which family members you want to be next to one another, or if you feel any members need to be separate from one another.

5. Will you use many different colors, only a few, or no color?

Place of Peace Relaxation Exercise – Family Version

1. Take a deep breath in while you silently count to four. One, two, three, four.

2. Now breathe out slowly for four. One, two, three, four.

3. Remember to breathe from your abdomen. Breathe in again. One, two, three, four.

4. And out again. One, two, three, four.

5. Now picture in your mind your place of peace. See that place in your mind.

6. Keep breathing slowly and deeply.

7. Let the muscles in your face relax.

8. Let your brow relax.

9. Let your jaw relax.

10. Let your neck and your shoulders relax.

11. Imagine all the tension draining out of them. Let it go.

12. Let your hands and arms go limp next to you.

13. Let your middle relax – your chest and your abdomen.

14. Keep breathing in and out.

15. Let your hips and your legs relax.

16. Let your feet relax.

17. Relax your whole body and imagine yourself in that favorite, safe place. Now imagine there is a giant bubble surrounding your place of peace. The bubble keeps you safe. It keeps the good inside, and the bad outside.

18. You get to choose what enters the bubble into your place of peace and what stays outside.

19. Now imagine any family members, including none, who you would like to invite into your place of peace. See them coming through the bubble to join you inside.

20. Next imagine any family members, including none, who you would like to leave outside your bubble, keeping them outside your place of peace. See them leaving your bubble so that only the people you choose are inside.

21. You feel completely supported inside your place of peace. You are fully in control of who comes in and who remains outside.

22. Breathe in to let in the safety and love you feel for those family members joining you.

23. Breathe out to push out any pain or discomfort.

24. Breathe in calm.

25. Breathe out any pain or discomfort.

Repeat the breathing process several more times.

Into Action

Continue working on your Family of Origin Collage and complete it before the next meeting. You will be asked to share it with another dad at the beginning of the next meeting. It may be helpful to work on it a little each night to keep any pressure off finishing it in time. Remember you can use the prompts starting on page 53 in this workbook to help you create your project.

Practical & Tactical

Think back to the children's family roles that were discussed in today's meeting: The Hero, the Scapegoat, the Lost Child, and the Mascot. Answer the following questions:

1. Which role do you feel was the primary role you took on in your family of origin? It is very likely that you identified with multiple roles but there was probably one that showed up the most especially as a child.

2. What purpose did you serve the family in taking on your primary role? What did your family get out of it? What did you get out of it?

3. What did your primary role cost you?

4. Describe the ways you continue to take on your primary childhood role in your relationships today.

5. Are there behaviors that help you still? Are there any that cost you still?

6. Do you see any of these roles playing out in how your children behave?

None of this is meant to shame you or be negative; it is just about bringing awareness and conscious choice to your behaviors. *YOU* get to decide what to do with that awareness.

Bonus: Have a conversation with someone in your family about your experiences. This could be your partner or someone from your immediate family. Ask them what role they think you would be. Ask them what role they might identify with the most. Discuss how these roles may still show up for you both in your relationships today.

Meeting 7 Summary

Our past influences our present. This may sound simple, but it's true. Therefore, this meeting focused on helping you explore your own history within your family of origin, learn some new ways to interpret your experiences in your family growing up, and recognize how those experiences influence you today. That influence may have resulted in you falling into similar family patterns as what you saw growing up, or it may have pushed you to do something different from your family of origin. Either option can be both good and bad. But the key to understanding the positives and negatives is *awareness*.

Awareness of what influences you allows you to intentionally choose your behavior. Maybe you will choose to keep doing what you have been doing because it is healthy. Or maybe you see that you have been acting in ways that aren't helpful to you or your children, and you now have the awareness and intention to do something differently. This is a gift you can give to yourself and your children so they do not end up having a similar experience to the one you had, if that is something you want them to avoid.

This is another meeting that may have been challenging for you, as many dads had very difficult experiences in their families of origin. If this is you, know that you are not alone. Also remember that you have access to many tools and skills that can help you manage any challenging emotions or reactions that come from what was discussed in this meeting.

Father of Mine

The primary focus of this meeting is to explore your relationship with your father. Many of us do not recognize our fathers as imperfect men with their own problems, insecurities, pain, and even trauma. Regardless of whether you liked your father or even knew him, he had a profound impact on your life just as you do – and always will – with your children. The hope is that this meeting will give you some new perspective on your father's life and communicate some of what you may have never shared with him to help you in healing or simply celebrating your relationship.

The goals of Meeting 8 are:

1. To explore your relationship with your father or father figure.
2. To recognize the roles your father played in shaping your life today.
3. To identify the expectations you and others place upon fathers and how that impacts your parenting.

Amazing Dads! Fatherhood Curriculum, Workbook, First Edition. Dan Griffin and Harrison Crawford.
© 2024 Dan Griffin and Harrison Crawford. Published 2024 by John Wiley & Sons, Inc.

Sharing Your Family of Origin Project

Use the following prompts to help you present your project to your dyad partner:

- Introduce the family members in your project to your dyad partner.

- Describe what made you choose this specific time in your life to use for your project.

- If you are not in your family project, why did you not include yourself?

- Describe why you placed family members next to or apart from one another.

- Describe your reasons for using the color(s) you used.

The exploration of your relationship with your father and/or father-figure is critical for your own growth to become the best father you can be. Many, many people have a "father wound" that stems from experiences with their father, whether their father was in their life or not. Sometimes the wounds can come from a father-figure who was not your biological father. No matter your experience or your relationship, exploring this in depth is part of you becoming a conscious father. If you have experienced a father wound, this can give you the nudge to begin looking at healing it.

Relationships with Our Fathers – Discussion Questions

In your subgroup, use the following questions to discuss your relationships with your fathers. Every dad should answer each question before moving to the next one. Make sure each of you answers each question in your discussion.

1. How would you describe your relationship with your father or father figure when you were a child?

2. How would you describe your relationship with your father or father figure when you were an adolescent?

3. If your father or father figure is still alive, how would you describe your relationship with him now? If he is no longer alive, how was your relationship when he died?

4. In what ways do you parent your children *similarly to how* your father or father figure parented you? Which of these are you proud of and which of these would you like to stop?

5. In what ways do you parent your children *differently* from how your father or father figure parented you? Did you consciously decide to parent differently than him?

Loving Kindness Meditation

1. Get into a relaxed position, for example, seated or lying down.
2. Take a deep breath in through your nose.
3. Hold it.
4. Now, slowly let it go through your mouth.
5. Let's do that one more time, please.
6. Take a deep breath in through your nose.
7. Hold it.
8. Now, slowly let it go through your mouth.
9. Continue breathing deeply, slowly, and steadily.
10. Focus on feeling kindness toward yourself. Move past any thoughts of doubt that come up.
11. Say the following phrases to yourself, not out loud but in your head.
    a. May I be happy.
    b. May I be healthy.
    c. May I know peace.
12. Continue breathing slowly and deeply.
13. Now think of a relationship you have struggled with. Picture that person in your mind.
14. Imagine that person as a child, before you knew them, before any conflict with them.
15. Say the following phrases to the image of this person you have in your mind:
    a. I wish you to be happy.
    b. I wish you to be healthy.
    c. I wish you to know peace.
16. Continue breathing deeply and slowly, breathing in kindness, and breathing out pain and conflict.

Amazing Dads! Fatherhood Curriculum

Into Action: Letter to Your Father

Write a letter to your father. You won't mail this letter and you don't have to share it with him, but it will be a chance for you to put on paper what you've always wanted to tell him. Take some time to think about what you'd really like to say. If you had a stepfather or grandfather who was the primary male figure in your life and you would prefer to write a letter to him, that's fine.

Spelling and grammar don't count; just write from your heart. Try to say the things that you have always wanted to say but were never able to.

You don't have to do this in letter form, either. There are many ways to express yourself. You can create drawings that reflect what you want to say, or you could create a collage, poem, a spoken-word piece, a rap, or share a song that expresses what you would like to communicate.

You may use the space provided to write or draw your message to your father. If you prefer, or if you think that you will need more space, do your writing or drawing on a separate piece of paper.

You may choose to share this letter with your father/father figure; however, carefully consider whether you and he are ready to have this experience. If you feel you would like to share your letter, consider waiting for a period of one month. Sit with the idea, and if you still feel that way in one month then explore sharing it. Perhaps even consider sharing it with a trusted friend, mentor, or sponsor and get their feedback.

The bottom line about the letter is this: Whether you do it as a letter or some form of art, you cannot do the wrong project, but you can do the EASY project. We instead encourage you to challenge yourself with this exercise.

Here are some prompts to get you thinking. These may help you write your letter:

1. If your father had a problem with mental health issues, alcohol, other drugs, or any other addiction, how did this impact you?
2. What did you learn about being a *man* from your father or father figure?
3. What did you learn about being a *father* from your father or father figure?
4. Do you think your father or father figure is, or would be, proud or disappointed in the father you have become?

Dear

Practical & Tactical

This week you have a choice of two options for this Practical & Tactical exercise. See the following two choices and pick one, though you could also choose to do both. You will not be asked to share these with the group, unless you so choose:

Option A

Write a letter from one of your children *to you*, the same way you wrote a letter to your father. Consider the following questions when writing this letter.

- What is it you hope your child will write to you?
- Are there things your child will wish that you had done differently?
- What will your child say you have done well?

Option B

Write a letter from *your father to you*. Write yourself the letter that you wish your father would write or would have written if your father is no longer alive. Consider the following questions when writing this letter:

- What have you always wanted to hear your father say to you?
- Is there anything he could write to you to improve the relationship you have/ had with him?

Dear

Meeting 8 Summary

Meeting 8 continued having you explore relationships with family and caregivers, specifically your father or father figures. For many dads, exploring this relationship can be quite painful, sad, or angering. Many dads have a "father wound" that exists and influences them as men and as dads. This meeting offered you a chance to explore that father wound by recognizing that your father or father figure was merely a man, with flaws and challenges, who made mistakes. Taking a detailed look at the relationship you had with him, whether he was involved in your life or not, is part of the healing process and builds insight into how you show up as a father. Perhaps you are similar to your father or father figure. Perhaps you do things very differently. Either way, your relationship with your father influences your choices.

Exploring the relationship with your father can be difficult, so you are strongly advised to check in with yourself and practice the skills you have learned to make sure you take care of yourself in healthy ways. This is especially true as you take the time to do the Into Action work of writing a letter to your father. It is best to give yourself time to complete the letter, so starting on it early is advised to allow yourself the option take breaks and come back to it if you need to.

Completing this exploration is a big step on the path to becoming a conscious father, and the father you desire to be!

Mothers

The primary focus of this meeting is to explore your relationship with your mother. Many of us do not recognize our mothers as imperfect women with their own problems, insecurities, pain, and even trauma. Regardless of whether you liked your mother or even knew her, she had a profound impact on your life. How you related to your mother and how she treated you is connected to how you relate to women and treat them. The hope with this meeting is to give you a new perspective on your mother's life and communicate some of what you may have never shared with her to help you in healing or simply celebrating your relationship.

The goals of Meeting 9 are:

1. To share our letters to our fathers with one another.
2. To explore your relationship with your mother.
3. To recognize the roles your mother played in shaping your life today.
4. To look at the connections between your relationship with your mother and how it influences how you treat women today.

This next activity gives you an opportunity to explore what "rules" there are for mothers and the different expectations that tend to be placed upon mothers.

Amazing Dads! Fatherhood Curriculum, Workbook, First Edition. Dan Griffin and Harrison Crawford.
© 2024 Dan Griffin and Harrison Crawford. Published 2024 by John Wiley & Sons, Inc.

Mother Rules and Expectations

You may use the following space to take notes during this interactive lecture:

1. When you think of a "bad" mother, what do you think of? Identify traits, behaviors, and weaknesses that you associate with "bad" mothers.

2. When you think of a "good" mother, what do you think of? Again, you can identify behaviors, strengths, and traits that you feel exemplify what makes a "good" mother.

3. When you think of your own mother, which of the responses to the previous two questions apply? Why?

Answer this next question in your subgroup, and feel free to take notes here:

4. How do the lessons you learned about women and mothers impact your parenting? How do they impact your relationship with the mother of your children?

Now that you have had a chance to explore the rules and expectations for mothers, it is time to delve more into your relationship with your own mother and/or mother-figure. No matter what your experience or your relationship is or was with your mother, exploring this in depth is important to give you perspective. It can also help you learn more about your perspective on the mother of your children, whether you are together, co-parenting, or no longer connected.

Relationships with Our Mothers – Discussion Questions

In your subgroup, use the following questions to discuss your relationships with your mothers. Every dad should answer each question before moving to the next one.

1. How would you describe your relationship with your mother or mother figure when you were a child?

2. How would you describe your relationship with your mother or mother figure when you were an adolescent?

3. If your mother or mother figure is still alive, how would you describe your relationship with her now? If she is no longer alive, how was your relationship when she died?

4. How did your father or other men treat your mother or mother figure?

5. In what ways do you parent like your mother or mother figure?

6. In what ways do you avoid parenting like your mother or mother figure?

Into Action: Letter to Your Mother

Write a letter to your mother. You won't mail this letter and you don't have to share it with her, but it will be a chance for you to put on paper what you've always wanted to tell her. Take some time to think about what you'd really like to say. If you had a stepmother or grandmother who was the primary female figure in your life and you would prefer to write a letter to her, that is fine. It is okay to feel anger or resentment toward your mother. It doesn't mean you love her any less or take away from the fact that she was there for you (if that was your experience). Nobody is perfect but if that resentment and anger is getting in the way of your relationships with other women, isn't it worth it to explore it?

Spelling and grammar don't count; just write from your heart. Try to say the things that you have always wanted to say but were never able to.

You don't have to do this in letter form, either. There are many ways to express yourself. You can create drawings that reflect what you want to say, or you could create a collage, poem, a spoken-word piece, a rap, or share a song that expresses what you would like to communicate.

You may use the space provided to write or draw your message to your mother. If you prefer, or if you think that you will need more space, do your writing or drawing on a separate piece of paper.

You may choose to share this letter with your mother/mother figure; however, carefully consider whether you and she are ready to have this experience. If you feel you would like to share your letter, consider waiting for a period of one month. Sit with the idea, and if you still feel that way in one month then explore sharing it. Perhaps even consider sharing it with a trusted friend, mentor, or sponsor and get their feedback.

The bottom line about the letter is this: Whether you do it as a letter or some form of art, you cannot do the wrong project, but you can do the EASY project. We instead encourage you to challenge yourself with this exercise.

Here are some prompts to get you thinking. These may help you write your letter:

1. If your mother or mother figure had a problem with mental health issues, alcohol, other drugs, or any other addiction, how did this impact you?
2. What did you learn about being a man from your mother or mother figure?
3. Do you hold any anger or resentment toward your mother or mother figure?

Dear

Practical & Tactical

Have a conversation with your wife, female partner, or co-parent about the expectations that are put on mothers. Discuss what you learned during this meeting as a way to explore her thoughts on this topic. Use this as an opportunity to gain more insight into her feelings on this topic. Here are several questions to help you in your discussion:

- What do you feel are the expectations put on you as a mother?

- How realistic do you think they are? How realistic do you think the number of expectations is?

- How do you feel if you judge yourself to have fallen short on an expectation?

- Is there any way I can help ease the expectations on you?

Meeting 9 Summary

This meeting gave you an opportunity to share your letter to your father with others in the group, and hopefully that was a valuable experience for you. We often think that nobody knows what we have gone through, but that activity often helps dads see that others have had similar experiences and that there is benefit in sharing those experiences together to promote healing. If your relationship was positive, then sharing that with the group was a beacon of hope for the other dads to recognize that *they* can be the ones to create that positive relationship with their children now.

You then shifted to discussing your relationship with your mother or mother figures. Similar to the previous meeting, this was a chance to look at your mother not as a divine being, although you may still view her that way, but as a human being with flaws, pain, and challenges of her own. Additionally, thinking about all the expectations that get put upon mothers can be an eye-opening exercise for many who realize just how unrealistic it is to pile all those expectations onto mothers.

Your opportunity to write a letter to your mother is just as important as the letter you wrote to your father. It's likely that this will be a much different letter than your father letter, in one way or another. But having a chance to express yourself to your mother this way, whether you end up ever sharing the contents with her or not, is part of your journey to recognize what influences you and express your thoughts and feelings about your experiences in one of your most influential relationships. As always, please make sure you check in with yourself and take care of yourself if any part of this becomes difficult for you.

Healthy Relationships Are for Us Too!

The focus of this meeting is to look at the importance of relationships in the lives of men. It may seem obvious that relationships are critical to a father's healthy life but our society still does not truly or adequately prepare men to be able to navigate relationships. In particular, you will explore the importance of repairing as relates to helping to deal with conflict that occurs with your children. You will use actual scenarios from your life and get support from your group members on how to show up differently with new tools, tools you should have been given all along.

The goals of Meeting 10 are:

1. To share our letters to our mothers.
2. To learn how the Man Rules teach us to disconnect from others and the impact that has on your relationships.
3. To learn how healthy relationships go through the process of connection, disconnection, and reconnection.
4. To understand the significant role trauma often plays in relationships with others.
5. To identify ways to model healthy relationships for your children.

Amazing Dads! Fatherhood Curriculum, Workbook, First Edition. Dan Griffin and Harrison Crawford.
© 2024 Dan Griffin and Harrison Crawford. Published 2024 by John Wiley & Sons, Inc.

Repairing is one of the most important skills you can learn for managing relationships and conflict. The Man Rules often impact our desire, and sometimes our ability, to respond to conflict and disconnection in healthy ways. As someone working towards conscious fatherhood, you now have the power to recognize the influence of the Rules and try to do things differently. Use this next activity to help you prepare for and practice how to respond to conflict in healthy ways and how to repair disconnection when it happens.

Repairing in Relationships

Think of a recent conflict you had with your child, significant other, co-parent, or another important person in your life. Answer the following questions about the conflict:

1. What event started the conflict?

2. What were the actions you took during the conflict?

3. What were the feelings you experienced? (Remember to Dig Deeper when you identify the feelings – anger is probably not the core emotion you had.)

Next is a breakdown of the different skills you can use when trying to move through conflict and repair any disconnection that occurred.

Descriptions of Key Skills

- *Digging Deeper:* Looking at a situation that caused disconnection and trying to identify what happened on a deeper and more emotional level. On the surface, it may just seem like anger. But as you think more about the situation, your reaction, and what you were actually feeling and experiencing, you move into deeper layers of what happened. This helps you figure out what emotion got dumped into the Anger Funnel and came out as anger, rage, and/or violence.

- *Being Small:* Recognizing that as men we are often bigger, louder, and intimidating to our children, especially in our anger responses. Being Small means getting down on your knees or sitting down when you're interacting with your children. Reducing the size of your presence makes you less intimidating to them. Get down to their level. Also, consciously try to lower your volume and speak in an even tone. This can change how you are perceived by your children and can help lower your own agitation.

- *Standing Up Gently:* This involves asserting your own needs, thoughts, and feelings in a way that is not aggressive. You identify the real issue and address it in a way that is effective and assertive. This addresses the conflict head-on rather than trying to avoid it.

Into Action

Step One

Think about your closest and healthiest relationship. This may be a relationship with one of your children, with your significant other, with a parent or sibling, or any number of people. Think of the one that you feel is the healthiest. Choose a song, poem, piece of art, or any form of creative expression that you feel represents this relationship. This can take whatever form you would like, and it will probably be an instinctive choice for you. *If you feel comfortable with this:* Play the song, read the poem, or show the person you have in mind whatever it is you chose to symbolize your relationship to them. Explain to him or her why you chose what you did, what it means to you, and what he or she means to you.

Step Two

Think about one of your relationships that is not that healthy, but you believe is worth the time and effort to improve. This may be a relationship with one of your children, with your significant other, with a parent or sibling, or any number of people. Choose a song, spoken word, piece of art, or any form of creative expression that you feel represents this relationship. Now, think about what you would want to do to repair and reconnect in this relationship. *If you feel comfortable with this:* Play the song, read the poem, or show the person you have in mind whatever it is you chose to symbolize your relationship to them. Explain to him or her the reason you chose what you did, and the ways you feel the relationship can be reconnected or repaired. If possible, make an agreement to work on the relationship together.

Practical & Tactical #1

In your journal, write about (or draw) how the Man Rules have affected your relationships with your children. In what ways have the Man Rules impacted how you interact with them, or how you approach your relationship with them? Talk to your children about what you wrote. Discuss with them the ways you can use the information you now know about the Man Rules to make different choices about how you relate to them.

Next, look over any notes you have about the Man Rules and how they conflict with what we have discussed are principles of healthy relationships. In your journal, write about how the Man Rules have affected your adult relationships. It may help to think about one particular relationship.

- Identify the ways your relationship with that adult has been impacted by the Man Rules. Talk to that person about what you wrote.
- Brainstorm ways you both can use this information to help improve your relationship.

Practical & Tactical #2

You may have experienced an emotional response during this meeting when you were asked to identify and role play a recent conflict you had. Perhaps that conflict is still raw for you. Sometimes the emotional response can come days later.

Take some time for yourself to write about this in your journal. Here are some examples of what you could write about:

- What is the emotional response you experienced or are experiencing?
- What do you think it means that you had this response even after the conflict?
- What can you use from this meeting or this program in general to address (a) your emotional response and (b) the original conflict in a healthy way?

Meeting 10 Summary

Similar to the previous meeting, you had the chance to share your letter to your mother with the group as a means of continued healing and connection with the other dads in the group. The remainder of this meeting broadened the scope from the specific relationships with your mother and father and focused on how to create healthy relationships more generally. Discussion of the Man Rules as they relate to relationships is critical because those rules usually push boys and men away from developing relationships, at least non-sexual relationships, with others. The effect this has is that boys and men grow up without having developed skills to create and maintain healthy relationships. Why would they develop those skills when the Man Rules kept telling them that relationships are for women to care about?

As a dad now, you surely recognize the importance of relationships: with your children, your significant other, your co-parent, and yourself. The good news is that you are committed to being a healthy father and that means you can learn the skills to help strengthen your relationships, or perhaps to recognize which relationships are unhealthy and need to be let go.

Much of the meeting focused on conflict and how to repair disconnection. This is critical because there are very few meaningful relationships you will have where conflict doesn't come up. Learning how to repair the disconnection that can happen during conflict is one of the most important skills for maintaining healthy relationships with anybody. If you can meaningfully repair and reconnect after conflict, you have the ability to preserve the relationships that are most important to you.

Communication Is Key

You cannot have a relationship without communication. That doesn't mean we do it well. A lot of communication is driven by our feelings, and we don't even realize it. This meeting will provide some guidance around the four basic styles of communication – passive, aggressive, passive–aggressive, and assertive. You will have the opportunity to look at the benefits and costs of each communication style. Then, you will get to practice one of the most important skills of communication: listening. Whether it is listening to your partners or your kids, it is critical this skill be developed as you seek to improve as a father.

The goals of Meeting 11 are:

1. To learn different styles of communication.
2. To understand that there are benefits and costs to each style of communication.
3. To learn that communication involves more than just the words you use.
4. To learn skills for communicating well with others.

This meeting is the first with some new breathing and grounding exercises that are part of the check-in process. You will find those new exercises on the coming pages. You can also find them at the back of the workbook in the appendix where all the grounding, relaxation, and breathing exercises are located in one spot.

Amazing Dads! Fatherhood Curriculum, Workbook, First Edition. Dan Griffin and Harrison Crawford.
© 2024 Dan Griffin and Harrison Crawford. Published 2024 by John Wiley & Sons, Inc.

Full Body Breathing

Begin in a standing position, making sure you have space in front of you for this exercise.

- Standing up straight, take a deep breath in for six counts through your nose. One, two, three, four, five, six.

- Hold your breath for a count of four. One, two, three, four.

- Exhale your full breath through your mouth for six counts. One, two, three, four, five, six.

- Now, slowly bend forward at the waist, keeping your knees slightly bent, and let your arms dangle down toward the floor. Bend as far as you are comfortable with.

- As you inhale slowly and deeply, return to a standing position by rolling up slowly, lifting your head last. Do this over the course of six counts.

- When you reach your full standing position, hold your breath for a count of four.

- Exhale slowly as you return to your starting position, bending forward from the waist. Do this for six counts.

- Repeat the process again. Bend at the waist, with your arms dangling toward the ground. Slowly take a deep breath and roll up to a standing position over six counts.

- Hold your breath for a count of four at the top.

- Exhale slowly as you roll back down to your starting position over six counts.

Now go through this routine two more times on your own. Make sure to do this slowly to help avoid any pain or injuries. Notice how it feels to stretch while you breathe.

Optional: If you have any pain issues, especially in your back, the following can be a less physically demanding version of the exercise.

- Start with your arms hanging down against your sides.

- As you begin to take a deep breath in for a count of six, slowly raise your arms in an arc until they meet above your head outstretched. The motion is similar to doing a jumping jack.

- Hold your breath and your arms outstretched for a count of four.

- As you exhale for a count of six, bring your arms down along the same arc until they are back at your sides.

This exercise combines the physical element of stretching with the same breathing skills as some of the other exercises. It is a good exercise to do in the morning to help stretch out stiff muscles and open your breathing passages.

Progressive Muscle Relaxation

The exercise involves tensing different muscle groups. If you have pain in any areas of your body and you feel that tensing that area would be painful, skip the tension part of that muscle group and focus on the relaxation of the muscles.

1. Begin by taking a deep breath for a count of four. Notice the feeling of air filling up your lungs. One, two, three, four.
2. Hold your breath for a count of four. One, two, three, four.
3. Release the breath slowly for a count of four and let the tension out of your body. One, two, three, four.
4. Pause for a count of four. One, two, three, four.
5. Even slower now, take another deep breath this time for a count of six. One, two, three, four, five, six.
6. Hold it for a count of six. One, two, three, four, five, six.
7. Slowly release the breath over a count of six, feeling the tension leaving your body. One, two, three, four, five, six.
8. Now, move your attention to your feet. Begin to tense your feet by curling your toes and the arch of your foot. Hold the tension and notice what it feels like. (*5-second pause*)
9. Release the tension in your feet and notice the new feeling of relaxation.
10. Next, shift your focus to your lower legs. Tense the muscles in your calves. Hold them tightly and pay attention to the feeling of tension. (*5-second pause*)
11. Release the tension from your lower legs. Again, notice the feeling of relaxation. Remember to continue taking deep breaths.
12. Next, tense the muscles of your upper leg and pelvis and hold it. You can do this by squeezing your thighs together. Make sure you feel tension without going to the point of strain. (*5-second pause*)
13. Now release and feel the tension leave your muscles.
14. Begin to tense your stomach and chest. You can do this by sucking in your stomach. Squeeze harder and hold the tension. (*5-second pause*)
15. Release the tension. Allow your body to go limp. Notice the feeling of relaxation.

16. Continue taking deep breaths. Breathe in slowly, noticing how it feels as the air fills your lungs.

17. Release the air slowly, feeling it leave your lungs on its way out.

18. Next, tense the muscles in your back by bringing your shoulders together behind you. Hold them tightly. Tense them as hard as you can without straining and keep holding. (*5-second pause*)

19. Release the tension from your back. Feel it slowly leaving your body, being replaced by a feeling of relaxation. Notice how different your body feels when you allow it to relax.

20. Tense your arms all the way from your hands to your shoulders. Make a fist and squeeze all the way up your arm. Hold it. (*5-second pause*)

21. Release the tension from your arms and shoulders and notice how your arms feel limp and at ease.

22. Move up to your neck and your head. Tense your face and neck by distorting the muscles around your eyes and mouth. (*5-second pause*)

23. Release the tension. Again, notice the new feeling of relaxation.

24. Finally, tense your entire body. Tense your feet, legs, stomach, chest, arms, head, and neck. Tense harder, without straining, and hold that tension. (*5-second pause*)

25. Now release and allow your body to go completely limp. Pay attention to that feeling of relaxation, and how different it is from the feeling of tension.

26. Begin to wake your body up by slowly shifting your arms and legs.

Holding tension in the muscle and then releasing it can create the feeling of full relaxation in that muscle. By going through all the major muscle groups, you can practice removing the tension from the whole body. Additionally, shifting your focus to different parts of your body is a grounding practice by keeping your mind in the present – the "here and now" – and noticing sensations in your body. As you practice this exercise, you will likely see an improvement in your ability to really feel the relaxation effect.

Being able to understand the common styles people use to communicate can help in many ways: you can identify the way(s) you tend to communicate with others, you can begin to recognize the ways others communicate with you, and you can be more intentional about how you want to communicate especially with your children and loved ones. You learned how the Man Rules also impact the communication styles many dads use – the Rules influence so much! Now, you have the ability to recognize their influence and make conscious choices to try and use the most appropriate communication style for any given situation.

Communication Styles

The following are four of the most common styles of communication:

- *Passive*: Dads who are passive communicators put the needs, wants, and feelings of others ahead of their own. This could be their children's, spouse's, or others in their lives. Dads with a passive style of communication generally go along with others to the point where they tend to agree to things they don't want to. This goes beyond a dad simply putting his children's needs first in an appropriate and healthy way. It involves avoiding communicating his own needs or important boundaries to avoid conflict, to his own detriment. Dads who are passive communicators may *believe* they are being treated unfairly but will not say anything about it. Passive communication seeks to avoid conflict at all costs, and the cost is usually highest for the dad who is being passive.

  Benefits   **Costs**

- *Aggressive*: Dads who are aggressive communicators often express their feelings and opinions with little regard for whom they are communicating with. This can be a dangerous form of communication. These dads are focused on being "right" or making sure their needs are met above anybody else's, including their children's. Aggressive communication can involve yelling, threatening, blaming, and even violent behavior. Unfortunately, this type of communication is often rewarded in the short term because others back down out of fear. Aggressive communication can give a false impression that it gets the job done, but the damaging effects, especially to children, are being proven more and more as studies show. Despite getting what they want, aggressive communicators experience real costs to their relationships.

  Benefits   **Costs**

- *Passive–aggressive*: Dads who use passive–aggressive communication appear passive on the surface but have little intent of giving in to the other person. They respond by acting out in more subtle or indirect ways. They may agree to do something, and then purposefully do it poorly, complain the whole time, or simply not follow through at all. For example, a dad might agree to give or do something for his child with no intention of following through. Or he might go along with his child's wish, like doing an activity, but complain about it the whole time. Sarcasm is often a sign of passive-aggressive communication. Dads who use this style *appear* cooperative but purposefully do things to undermine, annoy, or disrupt.

  Benefits   **Costs**

- *Assertive*: Dads who communicate assertively clearly state their opinions, feelings, and needs while still respecting their own boundaries and those of others. The assertive communicator does not want to avoid conflict at all costs, but he also doesn't want to overpower the other person to "win." This style is about making your needs known, but also listening to and respecting the needs of the person with whom you're communicating. Dads who use this style use "I" messages, which means they take ownership of their feelings and their role in the interaction. For example, a dad might say to his child, "I feel sad when I ask you to do something multiple times and it still doesn't get done," or "I feel frustrated when I am trying to talk and keep getting interrupted." This type of communication does not blame or shame the other person. This is the least emotion-driven form of communication of the four styles, and the most effective in the long term.

  Benefits   **Costs**

Next you will find examples of the benefits and costs of each communication style for you to reference.

You can use this to supplement the notes you already took.

Benefits and Costs of Communication Styles

- Passive:
  - *Benefits*: experience less conflict, avoid confrontation, "get along" with others
  - *Costs*: gets taken advantage of, needs don't get met, seen as a "pushover," low self-esteem

- Aggressive:
  - *Benefits*: your needs get prioritized over the needs of others, makes others back down, get your way quickly
  - *Costs*: harms relationships with others, people want to avoid communicating with you, scares people, seen as a bully, might provoke confrontation

- Passive–aggressive:
  - *Benefits*: seems like you are agreeing with the other person initially, sarcasm can make you feel good in the moment, avoids conflict initially
  - *Costs*: conflict tends to happen later after others realize you were not sincere, neither your needs nor the needs of others get met, people learn not to rely on you

- Assertive:
  - *Benefits*: allows you to voice your needs while still respecting the needs of others
  - *Costs*: can be interpreted as pushy or blunt, others may not know how to react to this style

Improving your ability to communicate effectively during times of conflict or when you feel yourself having a strong reaction is something that will benefit you in every relationship, not just as a father. However, the more you work at this and practice the tool below, the better you can be a positive role model for your children. Understanding that children respond differently depending on their age and developmental level, they are not likely to be able to use something like the PAR approach that comes next. However, by you modeling it for them, hopefully repeatedly, they will begin to "absorb" this as they learn what works best.

Pause, Assess, Respond (PAR)

Pause:

- Notice changes in my physical sensations, for example, heart pounding, sweating, or muscle tightness.
- These are clues to an emotional reaction or trigger.
- Pause the situation, take some deep breaths, get some fresh air, or take a "time out."

Assess:

- After the Pause, I can Assess the situation more clearly.
- Use the **TAMER** method.
  - *Trigger*: what event triggered my emotional reaction?
  - *Assumption*: what assumptions am I making about the event?
  - *Match*: does my reaction match the intensity of the event, or did my assumptions make my reaction stronger?
  - *Emotional Response* – consciously choose a new emotional response if my initial is out of line.

Respond:

- Put your new response into action.
- Make amends if needed.
- Communicate the process you just went through to the other person.

Communication is not just what we say or how we say it. Most times, communication is a two-way conversation so your ability to listen effectively and respectfully is just as important as how you speak. The listening demonstration in this meeting highlighted the impact that quality (or not so quality) listening can have on communication.

Active Listening

List the skills that are part of active listening:

Back-to-Back Drawing Activity

Sit back-to-back with your partner. Choose who will be the Speaker and who will be the Listener. The Speaker will be given a separate sheet of paper with a complex design on it. The Listener will have a pen/pencil and piece of paper. You should *not* be able to see your partner's paper.

The Speaker will describe the design to the Listener in as much detail as he feels is necessary. The goal is for the Listener to draw and recreate the design on his own paper. You will have five minutes to try to recreate the drawing. After the time ends, we'll compare the two papers to see how closely you were able to recreate the design. Then you will switch roles for the second round.

Questions for the Speaker after round one:

1. What did you do to try and make your instructions clear?

2. What was it like not having feedback from the Listener as you gave instructions?

Questions for the Listener after round one:

1. What did you like about the Speaker's instructions?

2. In what ways were the Speaker's instructions ambiguous or difficult to follow?

3. How do you think the outcome would have been different if you had been able to communicate with the Speaker?

Questions after round two:

1. Those of you who were Speakers this time, did you say anything specific based on what you learned from being the Listener?

2. Those who were Listeners this time, what feedback do you have about how hard or easy it was to draw based on the Speakers' instructions?

3. Which role was more frustrating for you, if any?

4. How well did you do in your pairs each round? How close was your drawing to the original design?

5. What we mean to say and how it's interpreted are not often the same. And communication is as much about being a good listener as being a good speaker. What steps can you take while listening and speaking to reduce misunderstandings in your real-life communications?

Into Action

Please answer the following questions:

1. What communication style do you use most with your children?

2. What communication style do you use most with your partner, co-parent, or other caregiver?

3. What can you do to improve your communication with your children, your partner/co-parent, or other family and friends?

4. Check in with your partner, co-parent, or other caregiver about how you come across when you communicate, especially during times of conflict and especially with your children. Share the four communication styles with him or her.

    a. Ask about the communication style s/he sees you using, especially during conflict.

    b. Ask for feedback about your body language, tone of voice, and volume.

    c. Ask if there is anything you can do differently to improve your communication.

*** Understand that the other person's response is just feedback, and you can decide to take it or leave it. The feedback does not say anything about you personally, but it offers you an opportunity to get information you might not normally get. Asking for this information during times of calm (not during conflict) can help you game plan for future conflicts, for example, reminding yourself of Being Small.

Practical & Tactical

Have a conversation with your children to come up with "Guidelines for Conflict" or "Fair Fighting Agreements" for conflict. It is also an excellent option to do this with your children and your partner, co-parent, or other caregivers together. Come up with a list of rules you all agree to use during those times. Ideally, write or print the list out and hang it in a place where everyone can see it.

Examples of Guidelines/Agreements:

- Use "I" messages.
  - "I" messages take ownership and do not place blame. "I" messages start off with "I feel. . ." and then your feelings about the conflict. For example, instead of saying "You always interrupt me, and it irritates me," you could say, "I feel frustrated when I am trying to talk and keep getting interrupted." The "I" message does not involve pointing blame. The message has more chance of getting through.

- No blaming.
- No yelling.
- No use of force, threatening, or intimidating.
- No name-calling or put-downs.
- If one person needs to cool off, give him/her time to do so.
  - Come up with a neutral signal for when someone needs this cool-off.
    - We suggest a neutral word or hand signal.
    - Can be any neutral word that has no real meaning behind it, like "pineapple," or a hand signal like the "time out" signal you see in sports.
    - This is something you agree on together, ahead of time, and when someone uses it during the conflict the others know to respect that it means the person needs time to cool off.
    - This helps all involved understand that the person needs a break and isn't just walking away.
  - Make sure the length of time for the cool-off period is clear, so you can come back to trying to resolve the conflict and the cool-off period doesn't last indefinitely.
- One person gets to speak at a time. No interrupting.
- Everyone needs to sit down while talking.
- Only the current conflict gets discussed. This is not an opportunity to bring up old grievances. If there are things that need to be addressed, that is for a future time that can be chosen.

Meeting 11 Summary

Similar to how the Man Rules encourage disconnection and push boys and men away from caring about relationships, the rules also place very little emphasis on the importance of being a good communicator. The messages we get early on tell us that "talking is for girls" and "men are bad at communicating."

These end up being self-fulfilling. They tell us we are bad at communicating so we don't put time into learning how to communicate and then guess what? We're bad communicators!

This meeting was designed to give you insight and tools to help improve your communication skills. You learned about the common communication styles and had a chance to explore the benefits and costs of each. The Pause, Assess, Respond approach was presented as another tool you can use to help you communicate effectively without getting caught up in the heat of the moment and letting an emotional reaction dictate the way you communicate. Revisit that idea multiple times so you can really get the hang of the process – it can help defuse difficult interactions. You have the process listed here in the workbook so you can review it whenever you need.

No discussion of communication skills is complete without including a discussion of active listening, so you got to see a demonstration of the difference it makes when someone actively listens to another person. Hopefully, you see the ways you can use these skills with your children right away.

Let's Talk About Sex

This is the first of two meetings dedicated to sex and sexuality. Given how much the Man Rules interweave masculinity, sex, and intimacy, it is vital that we explore these concepts in-depth. Your first reaction may be: "What does this have to do with me being a father?" More than you may think. Set aside your doubt, simply do the exercises and see if after you've gone through both meetings that you have a different perspective. This meeting begins with a very open and uncensored discussion about sex and sexuality – and the feelings connected to it that we often don't discuss. Then you will learn about the sex funnel and how sex and intimacy get confused a lot of the time. You will also learn how, whether you realize it or not, your life is full of intimacy. Finally, you have an opportunity to reflect on everything you wish you had been told and taught about sex and sexuality as a child, knowing what you know now.

The goals of Meeting 12 are:

1. To identify common topics related to sex and the feelings that we associate with them.
2. To define sexuality and intimacy, understand the differences between them, and learn how the Man Rules influence them.
3. To consider what you wish you had been told or taught about these topics as a boy or young man, especially knowing what you now know about sex, sexuality, and intimacy.

Amazing Dads! Fatherhood Curriculum, Workbook, First Edition. Dan Griffin and Harrison Crawford.
© 2024 Dan Griffin and Harrison Crawford. Published 2024 by John Wiley & Sons, Inc.

You might recognize the next image from the earlier discussion of the Anger Funnel. The Sex Funnel works in a very similar way to what you learned about the Anger Funnel. Feelings that are not considered "manly" are funneled out as sexual behaviors or thoughts. The Man Rules play a huge part in this because they do not place any importance on things like affection, intimacy, or even love. Instead, the Man Rules focus heavily on "getting some" and being a sexual superman. Once again, this impacts the experience that men and dads have in that they are encouraged to ignore a major part of the human experience in favor of simply seeking sexual gratification. The outcome is that men and dads do not recognize how they can experience closeness, intimacy, or love for someone who is not a sexual partner (or would-be sexual partner). Closeness, intimacy, and love are not solely connected to sex, but as a result of the conditioning from the Rules, dads are conditioned to limit their understanding of those concepts to being only about sex.

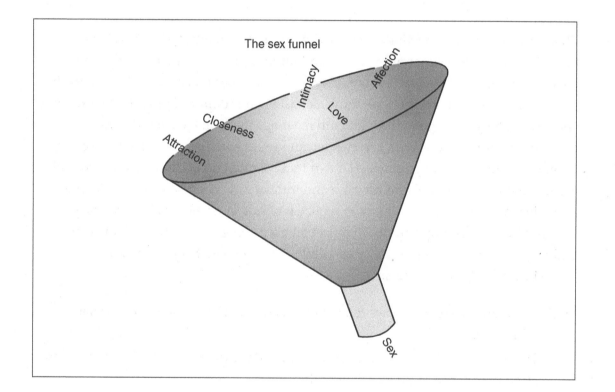

Sex, Sexuality, and Intimacy

In our culture generally, but primarily in the experience of boys men, the definitions of sex, sexuality, and intimacy get blurred together and confused. To really understand them, you need to have clear definitions.

- *Definition of sex:* Sexual behaviors; or the sex that people are assigned at birth.

- *Definition of sexuality:* An identification, a biological drive, an orientation, and an outlook. Sexuality involves how we act and with whom we act. Sexuality is not just about having sex but involves many aspects of the self.

- *Definition of intimacy:* An emotional experience of connection with another. Another clever way of thinking about intimacy is "Into me, you see." It is about allowing another to experience the real "you" through being open and vulnerable.

Types of Intimacy

Now that you have a clear definition of intimacy, you can begin to recognize how intimacy shows up in all kinds of situations and goes *way* beyond just sex. See below for examples of different types of intimacy.

- *Sexual:* Sharing physical and sensual pleasure.

- *Emotional:* Awareness and sharing of significant thoughts and feelings.

- *Intellectual:* Sharing the world of ideas; having mutual respect for intellectual capacities.

- *Recreational:* Sharing experiences of sports, hobbies, travel, and other fun.

- *Work:* Sharing common tasks; supporting each other in responsibilities.

- *Spiritual:* Sharing philosophies, religious experiences, and the "meaning of life."

- *Creative:* Being co-creators of a project; helping each other to grow.

- *Crisis:* Sharing closeness in coping with tragedy, problems, or pain.

- *Conflict:* Facing and struggling together with differences.

- *Communication:* Being honest, open, and trusting; engaging in positive or constructive confrontation.

- *Commitment:* Deriving togetherness from dedication to a common cause.

- *Aesthetic:* Sharing experiences of beauty, art, music, theater, dance, and so forth.

From Clinebell and Clinebell (1970). Copyright 1970 by Howard J. Clinebell and Charlotte H. Clinebell. Permission pending.

Subgroup Discussion Questions: Intimacy Exploration

As you begin to expand your understanding of intimacy and how it can show up in many different ways, use the following questions to explore further in your subgroup. There is space for you to take notes if desired.

1. In what ways have we developed intimacy with one another in our group? You can use the list provided for ideas.

2. In what ways do men experience intimacy?

3. How do different types of intimacy show up in your life?

4. How do you think this information about intimacy can help you improve your relationship with your children?

What I Wish I Had Known:

Using the space provided, write down the things you would like to tell the boyhood version of yourself about sex, sexuality, and intimacy. Hopefully the discussion in this meeting has helped you gain new awareness, new information, and new perspectives on these concepts. At the very least, you certainly know more now than you did as a boy. Think about what you would want to share with that boyhood version of yourself.

Perhaps you would tell him all the things you were never told by your father, mother, or caregivers. Perhaps you would warn him about certain things. What about porn? It seems to be everywhere these days. What about respecting your body and other people's bodies? What about all of the different feelings connected to sex and sexuality? You might want to share some positive experiences or aspects of your own sexuality. Maybe you would discuss some of the values you learned about sexuality. Or perhaps you would explain to him how the Man Rules will try to hijack his sexuality and how to recognize that. Write whatever comes to mind that you wish you had known when you were that young boy.

Things I would want to tell my younger self about sex, sexuality, and intimacy...

Into Action

1. How do you see the sex funnel showing up in your life?

2. If you were to change the way that the sex funnel works in your life, how might your relationships change?

3. What are you willing to change now about how the sex funnel works in your relationships?

4. In what ways do you show intimacy with your children that have nothing to do with sexuality?

Practical & Tactical

It is interesting to consider how different all our experiences of learning about sex, sexuality, and intimacy were when we were growing up. Some of us may have had healthy, informed discussions with parents or parental figures. Others may have had zero discussion with a parental figure and learned about these topics on our own or through friends, movies, and other media.

For this week's Practical & Tactical exercise, you are encouraged to find someone you trust and have a conversation with that person about his or her experience of learning about these topics when he or she was young. It is important to have this conversation with someone you feel is trusted and safe, and who feels the same way about you.

Here are some sample questions you could ask your trusted person:

1. Did your parents (or parental figures) ever sit you down and talk to you about the topics of sex, sexuality, and intimacy?
   a. If so, what was that like?
   b. If not, do you wish one or both had done so?
2. What do you wish you had learned about these topics when you were younger?
3. Do you think the depictions of sex, sexuality, and intimacy we see in the media are helpful or hurtful when it comes to young people learning about these topics? Why?
4. Would you be open to me sharing my answers to these questions with you?

The main idea behind this exercise is to begin to remove the stigma associated with having conversations about sex by helping you practice *healthy* conversations with others about these topics.

Meeting 12 Summary

This meeting was meant to introduce the topics of sex, sexuality, and intimacy in ways that you may not have experienced before. The Man Rules have a massive influence on our view of sex. Trying to discard the unhealthy messages you received over time about sex from peers, the media, and others is a tough task, but one that is worth the time and effort. Recognizing that intimacy is not just about sex and romance is often an eye-opening discovery for men. Again, the Man Rules pressed a very narrow definition of intimacy into our minds, but hopefully today gave you a chance to expand what you understand intimacy to be. You also had a chance to consider the messages and lessons you wish someone had taught you as a child or adolescent to help you learn healthier ideas about these topics.

Why is this part of the fatherhood curriculum? At the most basic level, sex is almost always required for fatherhood, right? How else did you become a dad (though we understand there is adoption, IVF, step-parenting, etc.)? Creating a healthier understanding of sex, sexuality, and intimacy will help you feel more confident when it comes to raising your children and helping them navigate these topics. Being a dad who feels confident in that will offer your children safety and security and will help you feel better knowing that you can give them healthy messages versus the messages they get outside of your parenting.

Let's REALLY Talk About Sex

In this second meeting focused on sex and sexuality, you begin by having an open conversation about how you learned about sex as a child. Then there is a very important conversation about consent that should be part of every academic curriculum. The meeting ends with you having the opportunity to begin to develop your very own "sex talk" with your children.

The goals of Meeting 13 are:

1. To practice healthy communication about sexuality in a safe space.
2. To improve your understanding of consent and the importance of teaching your children about consent.
3. To prepare for having "The Sex Talk" with your children.

Part of healthy sexuality involves understanding your own experience of learning about sex and sexuality growing up. You may or may not have had a healthy introduction to this, as every person's experience is often unique. However, part of conscious fatherhood means recognizing the positive and negatives of what you went through and then making intentional choices about how you want your children's experience to go. The questions in the next section will help you explore this further. Recognize that some of the questions might stir up some discomfort, bad memories, or be triggering. Remember the different skills you have learned to be able to cope with these feelings.

Amazing Dads! Fatherhood Curriculum, Workbook, First Edition. Dan Griffin and Harrison Crawford.
© 2024 Dan Griffin and Harrison Crawford. Published 2024 by John Wiley & Sons, Inc.

Let's Talk About Sex: Prompts for Subgroup Discussions

Answer the following questions in your subgroups:

1. Did your father, mother, or other caregiver talk to you about sex? If so, what was that conversation like? Do you want your kids to have a similar experience? Why or why not?

2. How old were you when you were first exposed to pornography? What was that like for you? What did it teach you about sex?

3. Would you want your kids to learn about pornography the same way you did? Why or why not?

4. With whom in your life would you feel comfortable having a "real" conversation about sex, if anybody? Have you had that conversation? How was it? What went well? What didn't go well?

5. What are you most worried about when it comes to talking to your children about sex, sexuality, and intimacy?

6. Would you be more worried about discussing sex with a daughter versus a son? Would it matter to you? Why or why not?

Defining Consent

Consent is a critical topic to know about and to be able to teach to your children, both boys and girls. Our society has done a poor job helping people clearly understand what consent is, who can and cannot give it, and how it applies to every person in any given sexual situation. Take the knowledge you gain during this next discussion and be sure to include consent in any conversations you have with your children.

1. How do you define consent?

2. How can someone get and/or give consent?

3. Who cannot consent?

Information on Consent

Definition: Consent is your agreement and permission to do a specific thing.

Getting consent:

- The clearest and safest form of consent is verbal consent, which is when someone gives clear verbal consent to do a specific thing.
- Nonverbal consent is another way to get consent, but it is not always clear, and the law does not always recognize nonverbal consent.

Who cannot consent?

Laws are different in every state. Make sure you know the laws where you live. Below are some general standards:

- Anyone under age 14 cannot consent to any sexual activity that involves a penis, vagina, clitoris, or anus.
- Anyone who is drunk, high, or otherwise impaired cannot legally provide consent.
- Mental and emotional vulnerabilities can also impair a person's ability to provide consent.
- Legal minors cannot consent to sexual activity if they are 3 or more years younger than the older partner, whether that older partner is a minor or not.

How does all of this relate to fatherhood and this fatherhood program? Being able to have healthy conversations with your children about these topics is one of the most important things you can do as a father. Imagine all the anxiety, discomfort, anger, and pain you can help your children avoid by being the person to give them *healthy* information. Imagine the comfort they will feel knowing that you are "in their corner" and someone they can turn to for healthy guidance and support when dealing with these topics that our society likes to avoid approaching in healthy ways. Think of the gift you can give your children through your willingness to be there for them in this way.

Preparing for "The Sex Talk"

There are many things you can choose to include in the conversation you have with your children about sexuality and intimacy. Here are some suggestions to help you organize what you want to say:

1. Topics I want to make sure I discuss with my children:

   a.

   b.

   c.

   d.

2. What topics am I afraid to discuss?

   a.

   b.

   c.

   d.

3. What topics feel uncomfortable or embarrassing for me to discuss even though I know they are important?

   a.

   b.

   c.

4. What might my children ask me?

   a.

   b.

   c.

5. What do I want to avoid?

   a.

   b.

   c.

6. What differences will/would there be in discussing this with a son versus a daughter? If applicable, why do you think there need to be differences?

Into Action

Continue working on what you would like to include in "The Sex Talk" about sex, sexuality, and intimacy with your children. Write down your ideas. Write examples of the things you want to say and think about some of the responses your children might have, or some of the questions they may ask you. Use the following space to keep track of your progress on this.

1. List the top three topics or "takeaways" you want to make sure you include in "The Sex Talk."

   a.

   b.

   c.

2. Write out more specifics about each of your top three – for example, what you would like to actually *say* about each one.

   a.

   b.

   c.

3. What can you do to make sure this is not a one-time conversation, but an ongoing dialogue with your children? How can you let them know that is what you hope for?

   a.

   b.

   c.

   d.

Practical & Tactical

It is never too early to begin to teach your children about consent. One way to do this is to give them the *option* of hugging or kissing people, rather than telling them to do it. For example, when you see family or friends instead of telling your children, "Give _____ a hug and a kiss," you can give them a choice: "Do you want to give _____ a hug or a high five?" This is a basic way to begin to teach your children that they are in control of their own bodies, and whom they touch and when. Subtle messages like these can help shape their understanding of the importance of consent.

Suggestions for Healthy Conversations with Your Children

There are many different suggestions and ideas out there for how to start a healthy dialogue with your children about this important topic. The following is a list of a few suggestions, but it is not a comprehensive list. This is meant as a starting point to help you prepare for "The Sex Talk" with your children. You can follow as many or as few of these suggestions as you like, but they are meant to set you up for success.

1. Approach this with an understanding that ideally this is not just one "Sex Talk" with your children, but an opening for ongoing dialogue with them.
2. Offer a safe space. Let your children know that you are open to talking with them about any questions, concerns, and issues about these topics.
3. Be willing to admit you don't know something. Consider the possibility of researching it with your children. This shows your children that it is okay to not have all the answers, and equally okay to seek the answers out.
4. Practice honesty, with discretion. Be truthful with your children, while understanding there should be some boundaries.
5. Roll with the discomfort. This is another good skill to model for your children. This does not mean pretending the discomfort is not there, but rather acknowledging it and showing your children that their needs are worth a little discomfort.
6. Discuss the Man Rules or Woman Rules about sex with your children. Building their awareness of the influence the rules have can give them insight and a glimpse at how they might make their own choices instead of unknowingly adhering to the rules.

7. Make sure you discuss consent. This is too important of a topic to forget about or avoid.

8. Talk to your partner or co-parent about what you would like to discuss with your children. Information about sex and sexuality can be confusing enough on its own, so you want to make sure you are on the same page as any other caregivers who might have a similar discussion with your children.

9. Understand that with all the media access children have today, you may need to consider beginning talking to your children at an earlier age than you expect.

Meeting 13 Summary

This meeting was meant to give you real, practical tools for navigating the concepts of sex and intimacy yourself, and giving healthy messages to your children, when the timing is appropriate. Being able to think back to your own introduction to these concepts is important. Perhaps you are content with how you were first exposed to sex and intimacy. More likely, though, it was not the healthiest introduction and you felt confused, uncertain, and maybe even afraid. Many parents don't even have real conversations about these topics, so boys are left to fend for themselves, learning from their peers and the media – less-than-healthy sources of information.

Your completion of this meeting is designed to set you up for successful conversations and healthy messaging to your children when it comes to sex and intimacy. A major part of that is beginning to consider what you want to talk about when it comes to the "Sex Talk." Starting to think about that now, even if your children are too young or you're not fully ready for the conversations, is one way to begin to decrease the anxiety you likely feel about discussing it. The more you put into this work ahead of time, the more confident you will feel when it comes time to have the Sex Talk and the more likely your children will be to receive it well.

Men's Health

In this meeting, you will explore what it means to be healthy in a holistic way. Physical health can often be overlooked for and by men. However, it is also easy for us not to fully consider all of the dimensions of health that impact our lives. That is why this meeting will have you explore eight dimensions of wellness. At the end of the meeting, you will have the opportunity to create your own comprehensive wellness plan so that you can give attention and care to the various needs in your life.

The goals of Meeting 14 are:

1. To explore how dads handle their physical health and wellness needs.
2. To identify barriers and challenges that dads experience when trying to take good care of their bodies, minds, and spirits.
3. To begin creating a Wellness Plan as a way of being intentional about caring for your own needs.

Amazing Dads! Fatherhood Curriculum, Workbook, First Edition. Dan Griffin and Harrison Crawford.
© 2024 Dan Griffin and Harrison Crawford. Published 2024 by John Wiley & Sons, Inc.

Eight Dimensions of Wellness

"Wellness is a holistic integration of physical, mental, and spiritual well-being, fueling the body, engaging the mind, and nurturing the spirit."
– National Institute of Health.

Take some time to explore the different dimensions of wellness, as well as the barriers you might face when trying to give attention to each dimension. Identifying examples will give you a list to choose from in the future when you want to do a wellness-related activity. Anticipating barriers ahead of time can help you explore ways to overcome the barriers before you encounter them.

Physical: Caring for your body to stay healthy now and in the future.
 Examples:

 Barriers:

Intellectual: Growing intellectually, maintaining curiosity about all there is to learn, valuing lifelong learning, responding positively to intellectual challenges, and expanding knowledge and skills while discovering the potential for sharing your gifts with others.
 Examples:

 Barriers:

Emotional: Understanding and respecting your feelings, values, and attitudes, appreciating the feelings of others, managing your emotions in a constructive way, and feeling positive and enthusiastic about your life.
 Examples:

Barriers:

Social: Maintaining healthy relationships, enjoying being with others, developing friendships and intimate relations, caring about others, letting others care about you, and contributing to your community.

Examples:

Barriers:

Spiritual: Finding purpose, value, and meaning in your life with or without organized religion and participating in activities that are consistent with your beliefs and values.

Examples:

Barriers:

Vocational: Preparing for and participating in work that provides personal satisfaction and life enrichment that is consistent with your values, goals, and lifestyle, and contributing your unique gifts, skills, and talents to work that is personally meaningful and rewarding.

Examples:

Barriers:

Financial: Managing your resources to live within your means, making informed financial decisions and investments, setting realistic goals, preparing for short-term and long-term needs or emergencies, and being aware that everyone's financial values, needs, and circumstances are unique.

Examples:

Barriers:

Environmental: Understanding how your social, natural, and built environments affect your health and well-being, being aware of the unstable state of the earth and the effects of your daily habits on the physical environment and demonstrating commitment to a healthy planet.

Examples:

Barriers:

My Physical Health

Physical health is one aspect of wellness, but one that many dads do not prioritize. There can be many different reasons for this, but the importance of taking care of yourself physically cannot be understated. The following questions are meant to get you thinking more about your perspectives on your physical health, your children's physical health, and any changes you are willing to make to be more intentional about taking care of you and your children's physical health needs.

To answer the following questions, rate yourself on a scale of 1–5 using the following scale as a guide:

1 = Not much, 2 = A little, 3 = Somewhat, 4 = A good amount, 5 = A great deal

1. On a scale of 1–5, how important is your physical health to you? _____

2. On a scale of 1–5, how well do you care for your physical health? _____

3. On a scale of 1–5, how much do you emphasize good physical health and exercise to your children? _____

4. On a scale of 1–5, how well do you help your children care for their physical health and create healthy habits? _____

5. On a scale of 1–5, how much do you encourage your children to participate in activities to promote wellness? _____

   Thinking about your previous answers:

6. What barriers or challenges affect how you are able to take care of you and your children's physical health needs?

7. How can you address the barriers and challenges identified earlier?

8. What do you plan to do to overcome the barriers you identified, or focus more on you and your children's physical health? Please write three specific actions you will take.

   a.

   b.

   c.

Into Action: Complete Your Wellness Plans

Now that you have a better understanding of the different dimensions of wellness, it is time for you to take a look at what you are interested in working on to improve in any of the dimensions you feel you could make positive changes or progress.

Consider any of the dimensions that you may not have put much thought into before. Or perhaps there were one or two dimensions that you immediately recognized as areas you want to improve in. The creation of a specific plan will help you identify exactly what you want to do in order to make progress in the area(s) you choose. The plan itself is meant to be a structured goal-setting plan. You can use this approach with *any* type of goal you want to achieve, and the process is broken down for you here:

- Identify a goal and clearly define what the goal is. For example, "get in shape" is too vague – "go to the gym three times a week" is nice and clear.
  - *Another example*: "I want to better understand my finances and create a budget."
- Choose specific steps you can take to make progress on the goal. Break your goal down into what needs to be done first. For the gym example, this could be "sign up for gym membership and schedule an orientation with a trainer at the gym."
  - *For budget example*: "I'll sit down and list all my bills out and then my income."
- Decide what timeline you will complete the specific steps. Putting a timeframe on the action steps keeps you moving forward. For the gym example: "I will go to the gym to sign up on Thursday at 9:00 am when I have time off work."
  - *For budget example*: "I'll create the list of bills and income information by Friday."
- Identify anything you need to help you accomplish the goal (for example, support from specific people and/or resources you need). Gym example: "I need a ride to the gym," or "I'm nervous so I would like my friend to come with me."
  - *Budget example*: "I need to get bill statements from a few companies to see what costs I have to deal with," or "My friend is excellent with money, I want to ask her/him for support."
- Consider what obstacles you might run into. This helps prepare you ahead of time versus trying to deal with barriers when they come up. Gym example: "I might not be motivated on Thursday morning, and I might want to postpone going," or "I might be really sore."
  - *Budget example*: "I am scared to learn what my issues with money might be," or "I will feel overwhelmed when I try to do this."
- Try to game plan how to overcome the obstacles you predict might come up. Gym example: "I will reward myself for going to the gym and signing up with (something that's not super unhealthy)," or "I'll get a heating pad and Epsom salts to help with sore muscles."
  - *Budget example*: "I will use a grounding skill to help ease my anxiety before I do this," or "I will focus just on getting my bills organized before looking into my income and trying to figure out a budget."

You are encouraged to use the Wellness Action Plan worksheet on the next page to really help you set quality goals and work toward the improvements you want to make. This worksheet is a helpful way to stay organized.

Wellness Action Plan:
Create an outline for your wellness goals

Remember the 8 Dimensions of Wellness: Physical, Intellectual, Emotional, Social, Spiritual, Vocational, Financial, Environmental

Goal	First Step	Timeline	Needs	Barriers	Solutions
What will you do? Write down your goal, but also the reason(s) you want to meet this goal, or the "why" of your goal.	What is the first step you need to take? Be as specific as you can.	When are you going to complete your first step? When do you want to complete the entire goal? Be as specific as you can.	What do you need to make this goal happen? Is there anyone who can help?	What is keeping you from reaching this goal? What could happen that would make reaching this goal difficult?	What can you do to take care of the barrier(s) you identified?
Goal 1:					
Goal 2:					
Goal 3:					
Goal 4:					
Goal 5:					

How will you know you have reached your goal? What are the results you want?

Goal 1: _____

Goal 2: _____

Goal 3: _____

Goal 4: _____

Goal 5: _____

Amazing Dads! Fatherhood Curriculum

Practical & Tactical

In the meeting, we talked about how important it is for you to model healthy habits and wellness behaviors for your children. For this Practical & Tactical exercise, you are encouraged to write down three ways you can use your example to get your children involved in wellness.

Consider what you might be able to do to involve them in activities that you do to promote your own health and wellness or come up with creative ways to work on this together. As you think of ideas, write them in the space provided below and then choose a timeframe to do the activities with them. Also consider the different dimensions of wellness and how you might be able to work on different dimensions with them.

Wellness ideas to practice with your children:

1.

2.

3.

When will you try each of the activities you identified earlier?

1.

2.

3.

Meeting 14 Summary

By this point in the program, you have heard numerous times that your children will do what they see you do. You are a role model to them, so modeling healthy choices and habits will increase the chances they make healthy choices and develop healthy habits. Meeting 14 was designed with this idea in mind: help you recognize how you can develop your own well-being so your children pick that up from you. There is an added emphasis on physical health because once again the Man Rules tend to direct us away from attending to our physical health needs. You deserve to be the healthiest you can be, and your children deserve that from you too!

Healthy Discipline

This meeting may be intense for you. We know that some people grew up in tough environments while others grew up in violent environments. There is a whole continuum of safety that boys grow up in. Some of you will have had the privilege of feeling safe and loved and valued your whole childhood. While others of you will have had experiences that would literally break some people. And everything in between. So, this meeting explores the difference between discipline and punishment. You will have an opportunity to learn about different discipline and parenting styles, which style(s) you use most often, and which one(s) you want to use more intentionally. We then ask you to take a very comprehensive look at abuse and violence in a way that men often do not discuss or explore. Take care of yourself and use the skills you have been learning in case you are triggered. And, as always, talk to someone and get support and help if you feel overwhelmed.

The goals of Meeting 15 are:

1. To define discipline and explore ways to use healthy discipline.
2. To learn how discipline can lead to abuse and violence in an effort to exert power and control.
3. To identify how to develop a healthy relationship with discipline, power, and control.

Amazing Dads! Fatherhood Curriculum, Workbook, First Edition. Dan Griffin and Harrison Crawford.
© 2024 Dan Griffin and Harrison Crawford. Published 2024 by John Wiley & Sons, Inc.

Defining Discipline:

The word "discipline" gets used frequently, but many times it is used to describe what is actually punishment. The difference is very important, so this is an opportunity to separate these two terms and get a better understanding of what they mean.

- Definition of discipline: Training that corrects, molds, or perfects. Discipline involves *teaching* and helping to instill good values. A noble goal of discipline can be to help your children learn "self-discipline" so they can recognize good values and correct, learn, and grow themselves.

- Definition of punishment: A penalty for a fault, offense, or violation. Punishment is a negative response to something that is perceived as wrong. Research consistently shows that punishment is less effective than reinforcement (positive responses to *good* choices or behaviors).

Now that you know the difference between discipline and punishment, feel free to take notes on what healthy discipline and unhealthy discipline look like based on the discussion in this meeting.

- Examples of *healthy* discipline:

- Examples of *unhealthy* discipline:

Parenting Styles

People are unique in how they raise their children, but there are some common styles of parenting that capture the majority of ways that parents try to interact with their children.

The following are three common parenting styles, described specifically for dads.

1. *Dictator:* The dictator style (also called authoritarian) is focused on getting children to obey and comply. There is little focus on teaching children self-discipline, problem-solving, or good judgment. Often, dads who use this style set overly strict and rigid rules. Many dads who use this style use harsher

punishment techniques, such as spanking or humiliation. One of the difficulties caused by this style is that the children learn to behave appropriately only to avoid punishment, and not because they value good behavior as its own reward. Another challenge of spanking can be that children learn it is okay to resolve interpersonal conflict through physical means. It can teach them that it is acceptable to physically hurt someone they love because that is what they experienced.

2. *Lax/Uninvolved:* Dads who practice lax discipline are often inconsistent, do not set firm boundaries with their children, and show little interest in teaching their children discipline or addressing misbehavior. The uninvolved dad may be around, but he is not concerned about what his children do, about correcting their behaviors, or about teaching them self-discipline. Sometimes the dad who uses this style is uninterested in his children's lives. Other times, this type of dad wants to focus more on being the "fun dad" and not having to be the one to correct or hand out consequences to his children.

3. *Firm-but-fair:* The firm-but-fair style (also called authoritative) meets in the middle of the previous two. Dads who use this style take a firm-but-fair approach to discipline. Rules and expectations for the children are clearly set. However, they are not overbearing and rigid, meaning children are given freedom to exercise their own judgment and learn lessons on their own. More critically, the rules and expectations are enforced *consistently*, and the children are taught the *reasons* those rules and expectations exist. Most of these types of responses to misbehavior involve discussion, coaching, and exploring different ways the children can behave that do not result in negative consequences for them.

Subgroup Discussion Questions: Healthy Discipline

Answer the following questions in your subgroups. Please be mindful of your own reaction to these questions as well as what the dads in your subgroup might be experiencing. Remember to use the tools you have learned to help regulate any trauma reactions, discomfort, fear, anxiety, or other difficult emotional responses.

Amazing Dads! Fatherhood Curriculum

1. How were you taught discipline as a child and adolescent? Which parenting style(s) did you experience? Was this effective or ineffective, and why?

2. How were you taught discipline as an adolescent? Which parenting style(s) did you experience? Did the style(s) change from when you were a child? Was this style (or styles) effective or ineffective, and why?

3. Which parenting styles do you find yourself using the most? What have you found to be most effective and least effective?

4. If you have a partner or co-parent, how do you coordinate your discipline with him/her/them? If you don't coordinate with another caregiver, what prevents you from doing so?

Small Group Discussion Questions: Abuse and Discipline

This discussion can be very challenging, so please remember to check-in with yourself and use any of the tools you have learned in this program to help calm and regulate yourself if you are feeling triggered, anxious, or any other discomfort. The next set of questions dives further into the topic of abuse, so be mindful of how you are responding as well as how your fellow dads are responding.

Answer the following questions in your small group.

1. What surprised you when you had to come up with examples for each type of abuse?

2. Do you know someone who has experienced any of these types of abuse?

3. Have you experienced any of these types of abuse? How did you feel afterwards? How do you feel now talking/writing about it?

4. Have you used any of these behaviors on your children? How did you feel afterwards? How do you think they felt?

5. What do you think is going on in a dad's head when he uses any of these behaviors on his child? What could that dad do differently beforehand to stop from using any of these behaviors?

Types of Abuse

The following are four common types of abuse, with examples. This is meant purely as a reference moving forward if you ever need/want to remind yourself of the various examples.

1. *Physical abuse:* pinching, slapping, pushing, hair pulling, spitting, restraining, shaking, kicking, choking, dragging, ripping clothing, biting, throwing objects, hitting with objects, slamming doors, kicking doors, punching walls, using one's body to block or intimidate someone, punching, burning, and stabbing.

2. *Sexual abuse:* sexual jokes, harassment, violating another person's boundaries, conveying inappropriate information, inappropriate touching, voyeurism, sexual hugs, commenting about developing bodies, reading or viewing pornography with a child, exhibitionism, fondling, French-kissing a child, oral sex, and penetration.

3. *Emotional abuse:* withdrawing, withholding approval or affection, manipulation through dishonesty, intimidation, and refusing to acknowledge the other's feelings.

4. *Verbal abuse:* name-calling, ridicule, constant criticism, blaming, threatening, and shouting or screaming.

Into Action

Answer the following questions. If you feel comfortable doing so, discuss your answers with your partner, co-parent, or a trusted friend.

1. How has your understanding of discipline changed? If it has not changed, describe why.

2. In what ways do you use or teach discipline like your parent(s)? In what ways do you do things differently?

3. What have been the most effective ways you have taught your children discipline?

4. What are some unhealthy discipline behaviors that you are willing to change?

5. How can you improve your coordination with your partner, co-parent, or any other caregivers regarding teaching discipline to your children?

Practical & Tactical

Spend time talking to your children about discipline. Ask them to explain how they perceive your approach and how effective they feel it is. Some example questions are listed here. Adjust the wording to fit your children's age and developmental level.

- When you make a choice that you know I don't think is ok or I will disagree with, what do I do that's helpful? What do I do that does not help?

- When you make a choice that you know I don't think is ok or I will disagree with, how would you like me to react?

- What do you like about how I react now? What don't you like about it?

- What helps you learn that a choice or behavior is not ok?

- What can I do to help you make good choices as often as possible?

Meeting 15 Summary

Before you continue reading this, take a nice, deep breath in through your nose, pause, and exhale it fully through your mouth. Well done. This program covers a number of difficult topics and conversations, and the discussion of abuse and discipline in this meeting ranks near the top in terms of taking a hard look at some challenging information. The takeaway of this meeting is meant to be that it takes real focus and intention to use discipline in a healthy way and to be able to draw a firm boundary around anything that is abusive.

You may have grown up experiencing some of the same behaviors that were discussed today. We ask you to remind yourself of this: *It is not your fault*. It's also possible that some abusive behaviors you experienced as a child or adolescent (or even adult) slipped into your own parenting. If that is the case, you need to recognize that those behaviors are now in the past and cannot be repeated. If repairing relationships is needed to leave those behaviors behind, then you have learned different tools to begin the repair process. Sometimes, this might require outside help and support. If that's the case, own that and lean into it. The reward is worth the effort. You have a special opportunity to change for the better. You and your children deserve those positive changes!

As someone committed to being a conscious father, you now have the information to guide you in your parenting so that you can teach your children discipline in healthy, effective ways. Being intentional about how you teach discipline and how you reward and punish your children is vital to breaking any cycles of violence or abuse that may exist in your history or your current experience. Mistakes will be made, but you now have the tools to limit those mistakes to "minor" ones. You also have the support of your fellow dads in the group and the facilitator(s).

Take care of yourself in the days to come. This meeting has the potential to trigger difficult memories, feelings, and impulses. Rely on the skills you have learned in this program, recognize when you would benefit from the support of others, and most of all remember the reason you are completing this program: to be the best father you can be. To be an Amazing Dad!

The Art of Play

How much time have you spent thinking about the importance and benefits of play in your children's lives? This meeting explores the research showing the importance of play in the lives of children *and* adults. You have the opportunity to work through some questions about the most effective way to play with your kids. And then, you get a chance to play! How cool is that? Enjoy.

The goals of Meeting 16 are:

1. To discuss the importance of playing with your children.
2. To share our experiences and successes in playing with our children so we can all learn from one another.
3. To learn how to use teachable moments during playtime to pass along skills you have learned in this program.
4. To have some FUN together!

Playtime is great! Playing with your children is something you probably thought of as soon as you found out you were going to be a dad. Even better, playtime has positive impacts on your children in many ways. Not only that, but playtime is good for you, the dad, as well! See below for some examples of benefits for children and parents.

Amazing Dads! Fatherhood Curriculum, Workbook, First Edition. Dan Griffin and Harrison Crawford.
© 2024 Dan Griffin and Harrison Crawford. Published 2024 by John Wiley & Sons, Inc.

Benefits of Play for Children

- Social skill development
- Physical development
- Helps develop self-control
- Helps develop emotional regulation skills
- Improves imagination
- Begins to teach teamwork
- Improves communication skills
- Improves child's gross and fine motor skills (depending on the activity)
- Helps develop leadership skills
- Reduces stress
- Increases oxytocin – the hormone related to empathy, bonding, and trust; this improves emotional, physical, and social health in children
- Forms closer bond with parents
- Helps develop resiliency – the ability to cope with challenges
- Provides frequent learning opportunities and teachable moments

Benefits of Play for Parents

- Increases oxytocin in parents – helps with bonding, lowers stress, has health benefits
- Bonding with their child
- Gives parents insight into their child's world and mind – interests, feelings, thoughts
- Helps parents improve communication with their child – some children may communicate more effectively through play
- Gives parents insight into how their child might learn best
- Offers teachable moments that can be very helpful to teach new skills – and since it's during play it does not feel tedious to the child
- Gives parents insight into their child's response to success, failure, and obstacles

How Do You Play? Discussion Questions

1. What are your favorite things to do when you play with your children?

2. What do you think are your children's favorite things to do or play with you?

3. When playing with your children, are you more likely to do what they want to do, or what you want to do? Why? Take some time and really think about this before answering.

4. Do you feel you have enough time to play with your children? If not, what's getting in the way?

Teachable Moments Discussion Questions

Playtime is great and the benefits have already been discussed. Part of the benefit of play is the ability for your children to learn important lessons and skills. As their father, you have the opportunity to, at times, help them recognize some valuable lessons and life skills through your interactions with them during playtime. Read the following scenario and then answer the questions.

Scenario: A dad and his children are playing their favorite board game. Dad pulls off a great move, but a move that hurts one of the kids' chances of winning. The child gets angry, picks up his game piece, and throws it across the room. This is a teachable moment. There are a lot of directions the dad could go with his response, and they all teach his child something slightly different.

- What are some of the ways the dad in the previous scenario could choose to respond? List any you can think of whether you agree with them or not.

- What are some of the skills we have learned in this program that the dad could try to teach his child?

Tips for Playtime with Your Children

- Actively observe, listen, support, talk, and understand.
- Give plenty of opportunities for the child to lead the play. Don't intrude and try to assert that things be done your way, but still be involved. Let the play be child-driven.
- Be emotionally supportive and nurturing, and show your child that you love him/her unconditionally. You can do this by being present when playing (e.g., not checking your phone or watching TV).
- It's not about doing fancy things, taking them to all sorts of elaborate activities, spending money – it's about interacting with them.
- Active play (being physically engaged) is more beneficial than passive play (e.g., screen time).
- Have unscheduled and unstructured playtime – free play.
- "If your child is smiling, laughing, or fully engaged with you then you're doing it right."

Into Action: Coat of Arms Prep

The following prompts will be used as part of an activity during our final meeting in which you will create your own personal Coat of Arms. There will be more of a description of the reasons behind this particular activity, but the goal is to have you use this Coat of Arms to represent yourself, your family, and who you want to be as a father. Please also involve your children in this exercise. Talk to them about the six prompts and invite them to help you come up with something or even have them choose some of them.

We want that final activity to be very meaningful to you, which is why you are being asked to work on the prompts below ahead of time. Please take your time to complete them thoughtfully and make sure to bring them to the next two meetings.

***This is not about your skill at drawing, but rather choosing meaningful symbols.**

1. Draw an animal that represents you.
2. Draw a symbol of your strength.
3. Draw a picture or symbol that represents your proudest moment.
4. Draw a picture or symbol that represents the most important thing you learned from your parent(s).
5. Draw a picture or symbol that represents the most important thing you want to teach your children.
6. Draw a picture or symbol that represents how you want your children to see you.

***For any of the above, you can choose to print or cut out a picture (e.g., off the Internet or from a magazine) instead of using a drawing. You will also be able to use magazines during the activity in the final meeting.**

Practical & Tactical

Look at your schedule between today and the next meeting. Consciously make time to play with your children each day between now and the next meeting. Even five more minutes than what you usually do is significant, whether that bumps it up to 60 minutes or takes it from no time to 5 minutes.

Write down when you want to make time to play with your children, (e.g., when you get home from work, when they get home from school, after dinner, etc.). Ideally, make time to play with each child one-on-one if that is possible. Writing these things down adds power to them and increases the likelihood you will follow through.

Meeting 16 Summary

"All work and no play makes Jack a dull boy." This is certainly one thing that the movie *The Shining* got right. It was time to have a little fun in this program. At the same time, you had the opportunity to learn about the benefits of play that go beyond just enjoying yourself and your kids. It's amazing how simply playing with your children is so healthy, both for your children and for you!

It is important to recognize that not every dad is in a position to spend time with his children right now. If that is your situation, our hope is that this meeting helped highlight the simple joy you can experience through play, and the benefits that *you* get from engaging in play yourself. Looking into the future, we wish for this meeting to give you hope on your journey to become the father you want to be for your children. When the time comes that you have the opportunity, play away!

A Balancing Act

Balance can be a difficult thing to achieve in our lives. You feel stressed by your job, parenting responsibilities, and everything else you have to do. This meeting is an opportunity to explore what healthy balance looks like and to understand that it can look different at different times. Sometimes it might not even be possible – and that is okay. At the end of this meeting you will have the opportunity to consider everything you have been learning in this program in a way that works and makes sense for you. We know that it can be overwhelming to have all of these different ideas and skills presented in a short period of time. This is your opportunity to not only make it manageable but also find an effective way to really implement it into your life so that it is truly time well spent.

The goals of Meeting 17 are:

1. To explore the ways you can manage all the competing interests and requirements that come with fatherhood.
2. To demonstrate and consider the benefits of having support from others in your life.
3. To create an action plan for how to find balance in a way that fits you as an individual.

Amazing Dads! Fatherhood Curriculum, Workbook, First Edition. Dan Griffin and Harrison Crawford.
© 2024 Dan Griffin and Harrison Crawford. Published 2024 by John Wiley & Sons, Inc.

Subgroup Discussions: Finding Balance

It is time to explore this topic for yourself and figure out how you want to define balance. Use the opportunity to discuss these ideas in your subgroup.

1. What does "finding balance" mean to you?

2. On a scale of 1–5, rate how well you do with balancing all the competing needs you have in your life. Why did you choose that rating?

3. How have your ideas about balance changed since having children?

4. What area(s) of your life do you think could use more attention right now? (*Hint: look back to the Wellness Action Plan you started working on after meeting 14*). Why did you choose this area/these areas?

Into Action: Complete My Amazing Dad Action Plan

Look through the list of topics, concepts, and skills we have covered in the *Amazing Dads!* program so far and choose up to three that are most important to you and that you want to start using or implementing in your life right away.

Step One: List up to three topics, concepts, or skills/tools you want to prioritize:

1.

2.

3.

Step Two: Get more specific – how do you want to use, practice, or implement each of the items you chose?

1.

2.

3.

Step Three: Choose one *specific* action you commit to doing over the course of the next week to make progress on each item you choose. Remember, avoid being vague and choose something that will allow you to know when you have completed the task.

1.

2.

3.

Step Four **(save this for the end of the week)**: How did you do on your action steps? Did you meet your commitment? If so, repeat this process for either a new set of skills or concepts, or keep the same ones you chose and just take the next step for each one.

Make notes in the following space on how you did over the course of the week on each item, and what your next steps are.

1.

2.

3.

Practical & Tactical #1: Identifying Supports

Support comes in many forms: a significant other, a family member, a friend, a group of other dads, a church group, a recovery group, various mutual support groups, and online support, among others. Take some time to think about the support you have in your life. Also, consider new supports you may want to seek out. Make a list in the space provided, and mark whether the person, group, etc. is a current support or a new one you identified. If it is a support you would like to seek out, briefly describe one step you can take to develop this new support. Over time, try to fill out the whole list so you have ten supports, a combination of ones that are active and others you plan to seek out.

1.

2.

3.

4.

5.

6.

7.

8.

9.

10.

Practical & Tactical #2: Activities for Balance

The following are examples of different behaviors or activities you can do to address different areas of your life. Take time to add your own ideas to the lists over time. The more you add, the more options you have in addressing each area to try and find your desired balance.

1. Create a list of self-care ideas:
   - Take a walk
   - Exercise
   - Read a book
   -
   -
   -
   -
   -
   -
   -

2. Create a list of fun activities to do with kids:

- Play a board game
- Color in a coloring book
- Plan your weekend or time off together
-
-
-
-
-
-
-

3. Create a list of fun things to do with a friend or significant other:

- Take a walk together
- Have dinner just the two of you
-
-
-
-
-
-
-
-

4. Create a list of fun things to do as a family. Focus on making them short and simple:

- Take a family walk
- Go to the park
-
-
-
-
-
-
-
-

5. Other ideas:

-
-
-
-
-
-
-
-
-
-

Meeting 17 Summary

You have so many competing interests that are begging you for time and attention; it is enough to drive a dad mad. Improving your ability to manage those competing interests in an effective way was the aim of this meeting. In our opinion, finding balance is more effective when you take moments to evaluate what requires your time, focus, and energy, and then you commit to meeting those demands. The tasks and responsibilities that require your attention most likely change from time to time, so this meeting was designed to help you get a better sense of how to shift focus when needed and prioritize the things that are most important at any given moment. We feel that the idea of giving equal time to all required tasks is not a realistic goal, so the ability to shift attention based on need is one that hopefully helps you feel less stressed and more confident in your ability to meet what is being asked of you.

We also recognized that this program has been an onslaught of information, tools, activities, and "assignments" for you to practice and complete. We have asked a lot of you! Being a conscious, healthy, and intentional father can be a lot of work at times. That is why we created the Amazing Dad Action Plan to help you clarify what you feel is most important to you and then choose specific steps you want to take to accomplish what you desire most. Once you feel good about what you have accomplished, you can always come back to this workbook and choose new concepts, skills, and exercises to focus on and practice.

*** Do not forget to finish the Into Action from Meeting 16 so you are prepared for the Coat of Arms activity that will be part of the final meeting.

Vision of Fatherhood

This may or may not be your last group meeting as part of the *Amazing Dads!* program. However, it is a powerful point in your journey where you get to really summarize the importance and breadth of the work you have done. You have been preparing to create your coat of arms for a couple of meetings now. Hopefully, you have included your children in the process of preparation if possible. Now you get to begin to create your actual coat of arms and share it with your fellow group members. Finally, because men are not always the best at saying goodbye or acknowledging their feelings for someone, you will have the opportunity to honor the connections you have made with the other Amazing Dads in your group in a special way.

The goals of Meeting 18 are:

1. To create a vision of the father you want to be by creating a personal Coat of Arms.
2. To acknowledge each other and the hard work and growth that has occurred in this group.
3. To practice healthy closure in your relationships.

Amazing Dads! Fatherhood Curriculum, Workbook, First Edition. Dan Griffin and Harrison Crawford. © 2024 Dan Griffin and Harrison Crawford. Published 2024 by John Wiley & Sons, Inc.

Create a Coat of Arms

You now have the opportunity to create a Coat of Arms that represents the different aspects of who you are as a man and a father. Ideally, you had a chance to get input from your children as part of this, but no matter what, this Coat of Arms is meant to be something personal and meaningful to you.

Here are the pieces you will use to put together your coat of arms along with the suggested placement of each piece. However, you can put them in any order you want on your own project:

1. Top left: A drawing/picture of an animal that represents you.
2. Top right: A drawing/picture of a symbol of your strength.
3. Middle left: A drawing/picture that represents your proudest moment.
4. Middle right: A drawing/picture that represents the most important thing you learned from your parents.
5. Bottom left: A drawing/picture that represents the most important thing you want to teach your children.
6. Bottom right: A drawing/picture that represents the way you want your children to see you.

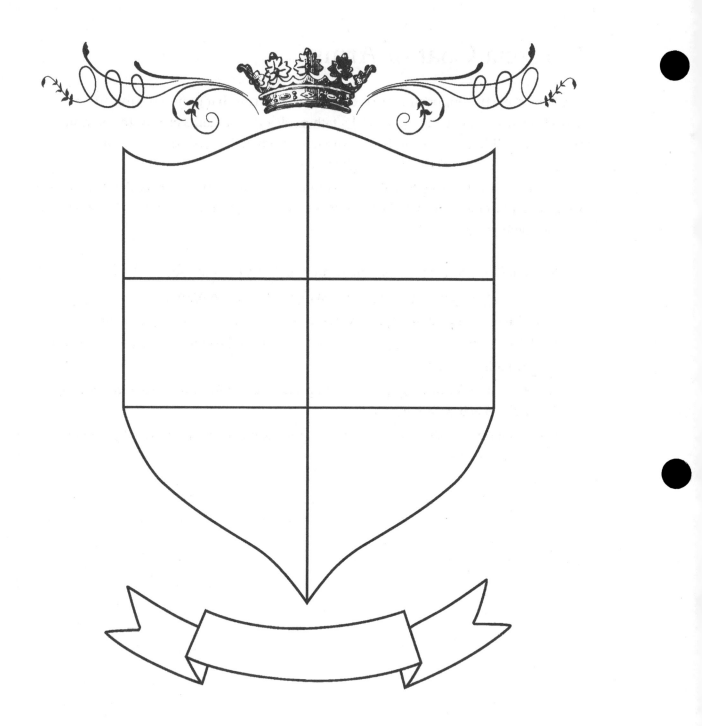

Meeting 18 Summary

What a long, amazing journey this has been! Take a brief moment to reflect on everything you have gone through to complete this *Amazing Dads!* program. . .

This final meeting is meant to be an opportunity for you to express how hard you have worked to be an Amazing Dad. The Coat of Arms activity was a chance for you to present your vision of yourself as you step into being the father you want to be. You can take pride in what you created, and we hope you keep it as a symbol of the work you did and the progress you made.

Equally as important was the opportunity to share your feedback with the other dads in the program. All of you worked so hard over the course of the program, and the connections you made here are ones that are probably unlike any others you have had to this point. We want you to cherish those connections and recognize the special group of men and dads you were a part of.

Reflecting On Your Experience

Please take a few minutes to answer the following questions and reflect on what you have experienced since you started this program. Congratulations on your effort and your hard work, and best wishes to you.

1. What are some of the things you remember doing in this group?

2. What are some of the things you remember feeling during the meetings?

3. What were the high points, or your favorite parts, of this program? Why were they your favorites?

4. What were the most difficult points? Why do you think they were difficult?

5. What was the most valuable thing you gained from being in this program?

Congratulations on finishing the Amazing Dads program!

Thank you for the time and effort you invested. As the authors, we are honored to have committed fathers such as you experience everything that *Amazing Dads!* has to offer. We sincerely hope that this experience has helped you learn about yourself and the father that you want to be. We also hope that you feel confident in your own abilities to use the information you learned, and that you will continue to see the benefits from your experience in this program.

Your journey to be the best father you can be doesn't end here, but you have achieved a huge milestone in that journey. Now it is up to you to continue learning, growing, listening, and teaching others. If you have friends who are also fathers, offer to share your experience and lessons learned with them. You can be an ambassador for helping the fathers around you grow in similar ways to you, if they want to, though remember that not everyone is ready to dive into this work just yet.

Please note that there is a QR code on the next page that will take you to a survey where you can give us feedback on your experience. We sincerely want to hear from you, so please check that out.

You can find more resources and information related to *Amazing Dads!* and your journey to conscious fatherhood on our website, www.AmazingDads.com. We also encourage you to come back to this workbook over time to refresh your memory, refresh your skills, and to remind you of all the hard work you put into bettering yourself!

Amazing Dads! Fatherhood Curriculum, Workbook, First Edition. Dan Griffin and Harrison Crawford.
© 2024 Dan Griffin and Harrison Crawford. Published 2024 by John Wiley & Sons, Inc.

Once again, congratulations on taking a huge step in your journey as a conscious father and an Amazing Dad, and please remember: it's not about using your skills perfectly, it's about using them consciously.

Request for your feedback

As the creators of Amazing Dads, we value feedback from anyone who has completed this program, and we would be very grateful if you could take just a few minutes to give us your thoughts on your experience.

Simply scan the QR code below and you will be directed to a brief survey.

We appreciate any feedback you can provide because we want to continue improving the *Amazing Dads!* program for future participants. Your honest opinions are of great value to us and will help shape future editions of this curriculum for all of the Amazing Dads to come. Thank you so much!

Amazing Dads! Fatherhood Curriculum, Workbook, First Edition. Dan Griffin and Harrison Crawford.
© 2024 Dan Griffin and Harrison Crawford. Published 2024 by John Wiley & Sons, Inc.

APPENDIX A

Grounding and Relaxation Exercises

Here, you will find all of the grounding and relaxation exercises that are included in the *Amazing Dads!* program. This section can be a great resource for you to return to when you find yourself needing a refresher on these skills. This is also a good resource for you to come to in times you want to choose an exercise and you can decide what fits your need in the moment. The exercises are shown here in the same order they were introduced in the meetings.

Box Breathing

This exercise can help you calm your body and your mind quickly and efficiently:

1. Put one hand on your chest and the other on your stomach.
2. As you take a few breaths, notice which hand is moving more. Try moving your breath deeper into your lower abdomen, so that your hand on your stomach moves more as you breathe.
3. Close your mouth and press your tongue lightly to the roof of your mouth. Let your jaw relax.
4. Take in a full breath slowly through your nose, counting to four.

5. Hold your breath, counting to four.

6. Exhale all the air through your mouth, counting to four.

7. Rest for a count of four.

8. As thoughts come up, acknowledge them, and then return your focus to your breathing and counting.

9. Go through three more rounds of this breathing on your own, slowly breathing in through your nose for four counts, holding for four counts, breathing out through your mouth for four counts, and resting for four counts.

Palms Up, Palms Down

This exercise can help you move aside anything that is weighing on your mind, or even any physical discomfort, in order to allow you to focus your mind on the present.

1. Sit up straight in your seats, with both feet on the floor and your eyes focused on your hands.

2. Hold both your arms outstretched, with your palms side by side and facing up as if someone was about to put something in your hands. Make sure you don't rest your arms on anything, they should be out in front of you in the air.

3. Visualize any thoughts, feelings, and stresses bothering you right now.

4. Now imagine placing all of your stresses, problems, troubles, and anything bothering you into your hands. These emotions and thoughts are out of your bodies and lying in your hands. Picture them there.

5. Go back inside yourself and find any remaining pain, discomfort, and stress. Then slowly feel these sensations move out through your arms and into your hands.

6. Imagine the weight of holding all these problems, difficult thoughts and emotions, and physical distress in your hands. Feel the strain of carrying them and the weight pushing down on your hands.

7. Now, slowly turn your hands upside down letting your palms face the floor. Let all the problems, stresses, difficult feelings, and negativity fall to the floor. For now, drop your burdens.

All these problems have not disappeared or been resolved, but you have chosen to put them down for the time being to be able to focus on what you need to.

In with the Good Breathing

Get comfortable in your seat. Concentrate on your breathing. Focus on your breath in, a pause, and your breath out. Feel your body expand outward with each full inhale and then return back to the center with each full exhale. With each breath, breathe a little deeper and move your breathing further down into your abdomen.

As you breathe in, take in positive things such as hope, courage, and love. As you breathe out, expel the challenging things you don't want in your life such as stress, self-doubt, and anxiety. Do this exercise for two minutes. Remember, breathe in the good and the positive, and breathe out the bad and the negative.

Five Senses Mindfulness

The Five Senses Mindfulness exercises is a simple and effective way to practice being in the present moment, in the "here and now." Find a quiet place where you can practice this for about 5–10 minutes without interruption. As you go through the steps, take about 15–30 seconds in between to give yourself time to experience each sense.

1. *Hearing*: Spend a few moments focusing on what you hear. Notice the different sounds, perhaps ones you didn't hear initially. Suspend any judgment of them. They are neither good nor bad; they just are.

2. *Smell*: Shift your attention to any smells you pick up. Again, notice them without assigning any judgment of good or bad, just that they are.

3. *Touch*: Focus on your sense of touch. Notice the feeling of the fabric of your clothes, or wherever your hands are resting. Notice the sensation of sitting in the chair, your feet on the ground.

4. *Sight*: Concentrate on your sense of sight by just observing what is around you. There are many things you could notice, from the different shades of color to different textures of the objects around you. Avoid judging the sights, and just observe them and then move to the next one.

5. *Taste*: Shift your attention to your sense of taste. If you have a snack, feel free to take a small bite. If not, notice any taste inside your mouth now, or the taste of the air you're breathing, again suspending judgment.

Amazing Dads! Fatherhood Curriculum

Place of Peace Relaxation Exercise

1. Take a deep breath in while you silently count to four. One, two, three, four.

2. Now breathe out slowly, silently counting to four again. One, two, three, four.

3. Remember to breathe from your abdomen. Breathe in again. One, two, three, four.

4. And out again. One, two, three, four.

5. Now picture in your mind a place of peace. Maybe you have been there before or maybe it is a place of your dreams. Maybe it's your bed or a comfortable chair. Maybe it's sitting by a lake or lying in the sun by the ocean. Maybe it's a special place you visited as a child or a scene from one of your favorite movies. It may be a real place or an imaginary place. See that place in your mind.

6. Keep breathing slowly and deeply.

7. Let the muscles in your face relax.

8. Let your brow relax.

9. Let your jaw relax.

10. Let your neck and your shoulders relax.

11. Imagine all the tension draining out of them. Let it go.

12. Let your hands and arms go limp next to you.

13. Let your middle relax – your chest and your abdomen.

14. Keep breathing in and out.

15. Let your hips and your legs relax.

16. Let your feet relax.

17. Relax your whole body and imagine yourself in that favorite, safe place. This is your place of peace. You are safe in this place. Your life is the life you always wanted it to be. You are the loving and caring father you want to be.

18. Your life is full of peace. You are full of peace.

19. As you breathe in these next couple of times, breathe in the word "Peace."

20. As you breathe out, exhale all the pain from your past and all the negative feelings and thoughts.

21. Breathe in peace.

22. Breathe out pain.

Repeat the breathing process several more times.

Exercise: Gratitude Breathing

Take a minute or two to identify three things you are grateful for in this moment. They do not need to be "huge" things. Even the small things are worth your gratitude. Write these three items down here:

1.

2.

3.

Next, make yourself comfortable and prepare to do some deep breathing:

- Take a deep breath through your nose, pause, and exhale fully through your mouth.
- Repeat this again.
- Now, with each full breath you take in through your nose, pause and say one of your gratitude items to yourself either out loud or in your mind.
- After you state your gratitude, exhale your breath fully through your mouth.
- Take another full breath through your nose, but this time as you pause with your full breath in, say another one of your gratitude items to yourself.
- Exhale the full breath through your mouth.
- Repeat this a third time, saying your third gratitude item to yourself before you exhale fully.
- Take a couple of minutes to repeat this same process until you have repeated each of your gratitude items three times.

Practicing gratitude can help build resilience. Even thinking about small things you are grateful for helps strengthen your "resilience muscles." Writing them down adds another layer to the positive effect that this can have.

This can also be turned into a cool activity to practice with your children. Have them practice gratitude – getting them to develop this habit now can have a big payoff throughout their lives!

Eagle's Wings Exercise

1. Take a few deep breaths from down in your abdomen.

2. Next, cross your hands across your chest so the tips of your middle fingers are just below your collarbone. The rest of your fingers will lay relaxed on your upper chest.

3. Try to have your fingers pointing up instead of outward. You can interlock your thumbs if this helps make it easier.

4. Now, slowly and steadily alternate tapping your hands on your chest repeatedly: right, left, right, left, resembling the flapping wings of an eagle.

5. Continue to take slow, deep breaths and continue tapping steadily

6. Notice what is going through your mind and body: whether it be thoughts, images, feelings, or physical sensations

7. Notice these things coming and going as you would watch clouds passing in the sky.

8. Continue breathing slowly and deeply.

9. Continue tapping: right, left, right, left, right, left.

10. When you feel in your body that you are relaxed, grounded, and it has been enough, you may stop.

Loving Kindness Meditation

1. Get into a relaxed position, for example, seated or lying down.

2. Take a deep breath through your nose.

3. Hold it.

4. Now, slowly let it go through your mouth.

5. Let's do that one more time, please.

6. Take a deep breath through your nose.

7. Hold it.

8. Now, slowly let it go through your mouth.

9. Continue breathing deeply, slowly, and steadily.

10. Focus on feeling kindness toward yourself. Move past any thoughts of doubt that come up.

11. Say the following phrases to yourself, not out loud but in your head.

    a. May I be happy.

    b. May I be healthy.

    c. May I know peace.

12. Continue breathing slowly and deeply.

13. Now think of a relationship you have struggled with. Picture that person in your mind.

14. Imagine that person as a child, before you knew them, before any conflict with them.

15. Say the following phrases to the image of this person you have in your mind:

    a. I wish you to be happy.

    b. I wish you to be healthy.

    c. I wish you to know peace.

16. Continue breathing deeply and slowly, breathing in kindness, and breathing out pain and conflict.

Full Body Breathing

Begin in a standing position, making sure you have space in front of you for this exercise.

- Standing up straight, take a deep breath in for six counts through your nose. One, two, three, four, five, six.

- Hold your breath for a count of four. One, two, three, four.

- Exhale your full breath through your mouth for six counts. One, two, three, four, five, six.

- Now, slowly bend forward at the waist, keeping your knees slightly bent, and let your arms dangle down toward the floor. Bend as far as you are comfortable with.

- As you inhale slowly and deeply, return to a standing position by rolling up slowly, lifting your head last. Do this over the course of six counts.

- When you reach your full standing position, hold your breath for a count of four.

- Exhale slowly as you return to your starting position, bending forward from the waist. Do this for six counts.

- Repeat the process again. Bend at the waist, with your arms dangling toward the ground. Slowly take a deep breath and roll up to a standing position over six counts.
- Hold your breath for a count of four at the top.
- Exhale slowly as you roll back down to your starting position over six counts.

Now go through this routine two more times on your own. Make sure to do this slowly to help avoid any pain or injuries. Notice how it feels to stretch while you breathe.

OPTIONAL: If you have any pain issues, especially in your back, the following can be a less physically demanding version of the exercise.

- Start with your arms hanging down against your sides.
- As you begin to take a deep breath in for a count of six, slowly raise your arms in an arc until they meet above your head outstretched. The motion is similar to doing a jumping jack.
- Hold your breath and your arms outstretched for a count of four.
- As you exhale for a count of six, bring your arms down along the same arc until they are back at your sides.

This exercise combines the physical element of stretching with the same breathing skills as some of the other exercises. It is a good exercise to do in the morning to help stretch out stiff muscles and open your breathing passages.

Progressive Muscle Relaxation

The exercise involves tensing different muscle groups. If you have pain in any areas of your body and you feel that tensing that area would be painful, skip the tension part of that muscle group, and focus on the relaxation of the muscles.

1. Begin by taking a deep breath for a count of four. Notice the feeling of air filling up your lungs. One, two, three, four.
2. Hold your breath for a count of four. One, two, three, four.
3. Release the breath slowly for a count of four and let the tension out of your body. One, two, three, four.

4. Pause for a count of four. One, two, three, four.

5. Even slower now, take another deep breath this time for a count of six. One, two, three, four, five, six.

6. Hold it for a count of six. One, two, three, four, five, six.

7. Slowly release the breath over a count of six, feeling the tension leaving your body. One, two, three, four, five, six.

8. Now, move your attention to your feet. Begin to tense your feet by curling your toes and the arch of your foot. Hold the tension and notice what it feels like. (*five-second pause*)

9. Release the tension in your feet and notice the new feeling of relaxation.

10. Next, shift your focus to your lower legs. Tense the muscles in your calves. Hold them tightly and pay attention to the feeling of tension. (*five-second pause*)

11. Release the tension from your lower legs. Again, notice the feeling of relaxation. Remember to continue taking deep breaths.

12. Next, tense the muscles of your upper leg and pelvis and hold it. You can do this by squeezing your thighs together. Make sure you feel tension without going to the point of strain. (*five-second pause*)

13. Now release and feel the tension leave your muscles.

14. Begin to tense your stomach and chest. You can do this by sucking in your stomach. Squeeze harder and hold the tension. (*five-second pause*)

15. Release the tension. Allow your body to go limp. Notice the feeling of relaxation.

16. Continue taking deep breaths. Breathe in slowly, noticing how it feels as the air fills your lungs.

17. Release the air slowly, feeling it leave your lungs on its way out.

18. Next, tense the muscles in your back by bringing your shoulders together behind you. Hold them tightly. Tense them as hard as you can without straining and keep holding. (*five-second pause*)

19. Release the tension from your back. Feel it slowly leaving your body, being replaced by a feeling of relaxation. Notice how different your body feels when you allow it to relax.

20. Tense your arms all the way from your hands to your shoulders. Make a fist and squeeze all the way up your arm. Hold it. (*five-second pause*)

21. Release the tension from your arms and shoulders and notice how your arms feel limp and at ease.

22. Move up to your neck and your head. Tense your face and neck by distorting the muscles around your eyes and mouth. (*five-second pause*)

23. Release the tension. Again, notice the new feeling of relaxation.

24. Finally, tense your entire body. Tense your feet, legs, stomach, chest, arms, head, and neck. Tense harder, without straining, and hold that tension. (*five-second pause*)

25. Now release and allow your body to go completely limp. Pay attention to that feeling of relaxation, and how different it is from the feeling of tension.

26. Begin to wake your body up by slowly shifting your arms and legs.

Holding tension in the muscle and then releasing it often gives a good sense of the feeling of full relaxation in that muscle. By going through all the major muscle groups, you can practice removing the tension from the whole body. Additionally, shifting your focus to different parts of your body is a grounding practice by keeping your mind in the present – the "here and now" – and noticing sensations in your body. As you practice this exercise, you will likely see an improvement in your ability to really feel the relaxation effect.

References

Black, C. (2018). Chapter One: Getting to Know Trauma In Unspoken Legacy: Addressing the Impact of Trauma and Addiction Within the Family (pp. 8–9). Central Recovery Press.

Clinebell, H. J. and Clinebell, C. H. (1970). The Intimate Marriage. New York: Harper & Row.

Amazing Dads! Fatherhood Curriculum, Workbook, First Edition. Dan Griffin and Harrison Crawford.
© 2024 Dan Griffin and Harrison Crawford. Published 2024 by John Wiley & Sons, Inc.